The Risk of the Cross

THE RISK
OF THE
CROSS

Christian Discipleship in the Nuclear Age

J. Christopher Grannis
Arthur J. Laffin
Elin Schade, CP

The Seabury Press / New York

1981
The Seabury Press
815 Second Avenue
New York, N.Y. 10017

Library of Congress Cataloging in Publication Data

Grannis, J Christopher.
  The risk of the cross.

  1. Peace (Theology)—Study and teaching. 2. Bible.
N. T. Mark—Study. I. Laffin, Arthur J., joint author.
II. Schade, Elin, joint author. III. Title.
BT736.4.G69   261.8′73   80-29281
ISBN 0-8164-2305-9 (pbk.)

Contents

Foreword   vii

Introduction   ix

Acknowledgments   xiii

Session 1   Who Is Jesus?   1

Session 2   The Journey of Discipleship   13

Session 3   To Trust in God's Promise   24

Session 4   To Risk Eucharistic Love   31

Session 5   A Liturgy of Life   38

Appendix 1   The Courage to Start   45

Appendix 2   The Nuclear Arms Race   51

Appendix 3   The Church on War and Peace   71

Appendix 4   The Human and Economic Costs of the Nuclear Arms Race   88

Appendix 5   Responding as Church to the Nuclear Arms Race   97

Foreword

Is there hope for history? This question, which was hardly asked in the fifties, has become an agonizing question for many in the eighties. The source of this anxiety is no longer just our individual or communal mortality but the death of all of history. Slowly a new consciousness is developing, a consciousness that has to come to terms with the possibility that history can come to an end.

It is this new consciousness that led Elin Schade, Chris Grannis, and Art Laffin to reflect on the meaning of discipleship in our nuclear age. They realized that because collective suicide is a possibility Christian discipleship has entered into a decisively new phase. To follow Christ on the way of the Cross, to leave father, mother, brother, and sister for his sake, and to lay down your life for your friends—these are challenges with a truly new meaning when the future itself has become doubtful.

Elin, Chris, and Art are not just three authors who decided to write a book together on one of the burning issues of our time. No, they are a woman and two men who have dedicated their lives to offering hope to history by all they do, say, and think. It has been a very great privilege for me to know them during the years in which they laid the foundation for this book. What has most impressed me is the movement in their lives from protest to prayer. The many protest actions in which they participated in the past made them realize with growing clarity that only a deep spiritual rootedness in the living Word of God would allow them to continue to say *No* to the escalating nuclear arms race without losing their own mental and spiritual integrity.

Slowly they came to realize that the value of their protests was based less on their ability to change the course of political history than on their vocation to announce the hope of the cross in the midst of a self-destructive human society. They came to see that the good news of the gospel is that Jesus Christ has overcome not only our personal deaths but also the death of human history. They came to understand that the challenge of the gospel is to offer hope in all places and at all times, and that their different actions for peace would be fruitful only when they are nurtured by this hope. The hope of the gospel is something other than the optimistic expectation that things will be better within a few decades, something other than the wish that politicians will change their minds, something other even than the desire to prevent the world from being destroyed by human hands. The hope of the gospel is based on the spiritual knowledge that love is stronger than death.

In this book Elin, Chris and Art offer the best of their most personal discoveries which they made during their struggle to find an honest as well as fearless response to the threat of a nuclear holocaust. In the Gospel of Mark they found a spirituality which enables them to be joyful even when the political situation looks quite grim, to be peaceful even when the sounds of war are all around us, and to be hopeful even when many people show signs of true despair. But they do more than just present the fruits of their own life in community. They also offer their ideas in such a way that those who explore them can find a new community themselves. Thus this book, which comes out of a life together, is also a book that leads to a new life together. It is therefore a truly Christian book. This becomes very clear when the authors point to the Eucharist as the basis and source of community in the midst of a chaotic fear-ridden world.

I am heartened by this book, heartened too by the way it was written, and deeply grateful for the hope it offers not just to individual people but to history as well.

Henri J. M. Nouwen

Introduction

Jesus tells us, "Fear is useless; what is needed is trust" (5:36). These words from Mark's gospel capture the spirit we wish to bear witness to in our lives and to express in this book. We have been called together by a faith in the power of God which is manifested in weakness—our own, and in that of others like us who struggle to confront the violent despair of the nuclear arms race with a message of Christian hope.

This book is the fruit of the Kingdom of God mysteriously at work in our midst. We, the writers, come from communities of faith nourished by the Word of God and the Eucharist. In our prayer together, we have been deeply stirred by the vulnerable, forgiving love of Jesus powerfully expressed on the Cross. His nonviolent example in the face of the consummate evil and blatant injustices of his day informs our struggles as his twentieth-century disciples. As people striving to follow his way we reject the arms race—both conventional and nuclear—as being diametrically opposed to Christ's Kingdom and his way of salvation through willing self-sacrifice.

One of our primary goals in writing the discussion articles is to discover, and to help others discover, the contemporary meaning of discipleship. In contrast to the other evangelists, Mark portrays the disciples in a largely critical light. They appear sincere but blind and misguided; they struggle for power among themselves and resist Christ's message of the Cross. Thus Mark's presentation of discipleship—a central theme of his gospel—is a study about struggle and human failure, not a study of heroic, faithful obedience. Mark's description of the disciples' failure lends itself well to an honest examination of our own faith and moral attitudes. In view of the generally unquestioning consent Christians give to the nuclear arms race, Mark's exposition of the meaning of true discipleship strongly recommends itself.

Mark uses a literary technique which reinforces the contrast between true and false discipleship. He frames or juxtaposes various accounts of Jesus' healing, teaching, and feeding—the range of his life-promoting actions—with contrasting accounts of behavior by others that are life-denying. For example, the healing of the two blind men before and after Jesus' three predictions of his death and resurrection highlights the spiritual blindness of the disciples who are incapable of comprehending the real significance of these predictions. The first four sessions in the book are organized around particular Markan frames. We have adopted Mark's framing technique as our own and have extended it to the contemporary situation, framing with the example of Jesus' life and teaching questions concerning the build-up of nuclear weapons.

We have tried to stay close to this gospel, to imitate Mark's evocative yet compact style. And as much as possible we have avoided both theological and political concepts that would distract the reader from the central question of discipleship.

We write as Americans about an urgent issue facing our society, but it is the quality of the human problem, not the national one, that we wish to examine. Our concern is global and encompasses the whole human family. We confront not merely the American or Soviet mentality, its weapons and technology, but more importantly the human fear and moral failure which is universal, and which lies beneath all motives of violence.

What distinguishes this work, we believe, from others that treat the problem of nuclear weapons in a gospel context, is our effort to interrelate the question of conscience with the question of faith. We are not presenting just an ethical argument on pacificism in the nuclear age; we are inviting as well a leap of faith, the intimate moment of repentance and conversion.

Such a moment flows from a pattern of human experience that is described throughout Mark's gospel—the pattern of perceiving and responding to the authority of Christ. The perception theme developed in the earlier sessions moves from the initial question of "Who is Jesus?" to the problem of discipleship as the journey to the Cross, and then to the contemporary problem of blindness to the full implications of nuclear weapons. The later sessions treat the faith and moral responses respectively, while the final gathering—in liturgy—celebrates the response of hope. This liturgy of the Word and Eucharist (session 5) culminates the search and reflection process of the previous four sessions and inaugurates a new commitment to faith and struggle.

Prayer and community are integral aspects of the Christian life. Sharing prayer establishes community; building community is itself a prayer. Both aspects together enable dynamic growth, a process based on relationships of trust. This book has grown out of such a process and, we hope, will help others to grow and yield fruit if used in the same way. We encourage a careful, contemplative attitude of prayer during the course of the sessions as well as an open, sensitive sharing among the members of the group. The questions of faith which are posed do not lend themselves to easy or immediate answers. A genuine trust in the Spirit and in one another is needed in order to face these questions honestly and to enable moments of repentance and conversion.

Suggestions for Group Use

While the book may be used for individual reflection—we would encourage that!—the overall format is designed to assist both new and established prayer and gospel-study groups. For new groups, we recommend an initial gathering, perhaps for a meal and personal introductions, before undertaking the first session together.

The basic gospel-study section consists of five sessions. Ideally, these would be scheduled on a consecutive weekly basis. The length of each session can vary from one and one-half to three hours depending upon the needs or limitations of the group. The first four sessions consist of the following elements with suggested time allotments for a two hour session:

Session Elements	*Suggested Time Allotment*
Opening Prayer ⎱ Reading from Mark ⎰	10 minutes
Review of the Articles	20 minutes
Discussion of Questions	1 hour
Evaluation and Planning	15 minutes
Closing Prayer	15 minutes

We encourage the designation of a facilitator for each session to ensure a smooth and fair process, and recommend that this role be shared or rotated among the members of the group. The facilitator is expected to invite introductions when necessary, to arrange for the opening prayer and the reading aloud of the Mark passage, to focus and moderate the group discussion, and to keep track of the time. Each participant, of course, shares responsibility for maintaining a focused and productive discussion and reflection.

The material provided for each session should be prepared before the gathering. The opening prayer and the Mark reading should be read aloud clearly and very slowly by someone familiar with the text. Silence is an important complement to these reflective readings.

For a fruitful discussion we recommend that the articles for discussion be read at least twice and the discussion questions be prepared before the session gathering. A twenty-minute review period during each session is suggested.

Allowing time at the close of each session for some group evaluation and planning is an important way of examining the process and dynamics within the group, of accounting for needs met or unmet, and of ensuring an adequate preparation for the next session.

The prayer closing each session begins with reflection on verses selected from the Mark reading. This can be followed by a period of spontaneous personal prayer and can conclude with a song or prayer familiar to all. This occasion should not be slighted because of time considerations. Again we affirm the importance of prayer within the group experience—its virtue in enabling growth cannot be underestimated.

The appendices of this book serve as a very important supplement to each of the five sessions. They contain a wide range of historical, political, and economic data on the nuclear arms race. The appendices also include religious and moral statements on peace and nuclear disarmament issued by groups and individuals, ways in which churches and Christian groups can become more active peacemakers, a list of groups working on national and local levels for justice and peace, books and magazines on pacifism and nuclear disarmament, and a variety of audio-visual aids. The appendix section is organized for use concurrently with the discussion articles and discussion questions. Each corresponding appendix should be read by the group prior to the session gatherings. Appendix 1, "The Courage to Start" by Robert Aldridge, should be read in preparation for the first session.

Acknowledgments

We are grateful to many people in and outside of our communities for their strong support and encouragement in the preparation of this book. Dean Hammer offered invaluable insights and suggestions in shaping this work, encouraging us continually to adhere to Mark's gospel and to bring out the basic themes and flavor of the evangelist's account. During the preparation of this book Dean, with seven of our friends, was arrested and jailed for a nonviolent act of resistance at a nuclear weapons plant. His involvement with this book and his deep appreciation of the gospel has informed and strengthened the integrity of his civil disobedience. His faith-filled action as one of the "Plough-shares 8", in turn, becomes a part of the book, an unwritten session on commitment, hope, and resistance. His contribution has been most significant.

We feel a special indebtedness to Father Edmund Nadolny of the Hartford Archdiocese Evangelization Office who enabled our initial work together and has continuously expressed interest in the progress of this book.

Kathryn Johnson and Joan Hofmann deserve many thanks for their encouragement and patient help in the preparation of the manuscript; their editing and typing skills were much appreciated. Bob Forsberg and Hud Richard also supported us with their characteristic servant-hood and continuing prayers.

We wish to thank as well two Christian communities whose hospitality and service created a peaceful and holy setting. Elin's community of Passionist Sisters at Our Lady of Calvary Retreat House in Farmington, Connecticut, has been extraordinarily generous in welcoming us for visits that always seemed to extend themselves. Likewise, our Christian brothers of the LaSalette Community in Cheshire, Connecticut, offered us kind hospitality for which we are grateful.

Lastly, we thank our friend Henri Nouwen, for his encouragement throughout the writing process. Most importantly, he has helped us to experience a deeper sense of reverence for the eucharist and for the healing it bestows, a healing that is central to the hope of this book.

J. Christopher Grannis
Arthur J. Laffin
Sr. Elin Schade

New Haven, October 1980

SESSION 1

Who Is Jesus?

Opening Prayer

Lord Jesus, we gather in your name to be healed and taught by you. In a world marred by manifest evils: starvation, poverty, war, disease, prejudice, crime, and the violence of lethal armaments, we recognize you as the One who can forgive our sins. You know our human condition, the often contradictory longings of our hearts, and the powerlessness we feel in the face of such complex and pervasive evil. You know us as both victim and perpetrator, and still you offer us your healing and intimacy. We rejoice that you "have come for sinners, not the self-righteous," because we know our need of you. Extend your reign in our hearts, teach us divine standards of judging and acting, and help us become new vessels of your Spirit. We ask this for the glory of your name. Amen.

Gospel Reading: Mark 2:1–3:6
(For a shorter reading: 2:13–2:22)

2 A PARALYTIC AT CAPERNAUM. [1] He came back to Capernaum after a lapse of several days and word got around that he was at home. [2] At that they began to gather in great numbers. There was no longer any room for them, even around the door. [3] While he was delivering God's word to them, some people arrived bringing a paralyzed man to him. The four who carried him [4] were unable to bring him to Jesus because of the crowd, so they began to open up the roof over the spot where Jesus was. When they had made a hole, they let down the mat on which the paralytic was lying. [5] When Jesus saw their faith, he said to the paralyzed man, "My son, your sins are forgiven." [6] Now some of the scribes were sitting there asking themselves: [7] "Why does the man talk in that way? He commits blasphemy! Who can forgive sins except God alone?" [8] Jesus was immediately aware of their reasoning, though they kept it to themselves, and he said to them: "Why do you harbor

1

these thoughts? [9]Which is easier, to say to the paralytic, 'Your sins are forgiven', or to say, 'Stand up, pick up your mat, and walk again'? [10]That you may know that the Son of man has authority on earth to forgive sins'' (he said to the paralyzed man), [11]''I command you: Stand up! Pick up your mat and go home.'' [12]The man stood and picked up his mat and went outside in the sight of everyone. They were awestruck; all gave praise to God, saying, ''We have never seen anything like this!''

THE CALL OF LEVI. [13]Another time, while he went walking along the lakeshore, people kept coming to him in crowds and he taught them. [14]As he moved on he saw Levi, the son of Alphaeus, at his tax collector's post, and said to him, ''Follow me.'' Levi got up and became his follower. [15]While Jesus was reclining to eat in Levi's house, many tax collectors and those known as sinners joined him and his disciples at dinner. The number of those who followed him was large. [16]When the scribes who belonged to the Pharisee party saw that he was eating with tax collectors and offenders against the law, they complained to his disciples, ''Why does he eat with such as these?'' [17]Overhearing the remark, Jesus said to them, ''People who are healthy do not need a doctor; sick people do. I have come to call sinners, not the self-righteous.''

THE QUESTION OF FASTING. [18]Now John's disciples and the Pharisees were accustomed to fast. People came to Jesus with the objection, ''Why do John's disciples and those of the Pharisees fast while yours do not?'' [19]Jesus replied: ''How can the guests at a wedding fast as long as the groom is still among them? So long as the groom stays with them, they cannot fast. [20]The day will come, however, when the groom will be taken away from them: on that day they will fast. [21]No one sews a patch of unshrunken cloth on an old cloak. If he should do so, the very thing he has used to cover the hole would pull away—the new from the old—and the tear would get worse. [22]Similarly, no man pours new wine into old wineskins. If he does so, the wine will burst the skins and both wine and skins will be lost. No, new wine is poured into new skins.''

THE DISCIPLES AND THE SABBATH. [23]It happened that he was walking through standing grain on the sabbath, and his disciples began to pull off heads of grain as they went along. [24]At this the Pharisees protested: "Look! Why do they do a thing not permitted on the sabbath?" 25 He said to them: "Have you never read what David did when he was in need and he and his men were hungry? 26 How he entered God's house in the days of Abiathar the high priest and ate the holy bread which only the priests were permitted to eat? He even gave it to his men." 27 Then he said to them: "The sabbath was made for man, not man for the sabbath. 28 That is why the Son of Man is lord even of the sabbath."

3 A MAN WITH A WITHERED HAND. 1 He returned to the synagogue where there was a man whose hand was shriveled up 2 They kept an eye on Jesus to see whether he would heal him on the sabbath, hoping to be able to bring an accusation against him. 3 He addressed the man with the shriveled hand: "Stand up here in front!" 4 Then he said to them: "Is it permitted to do a good deed on the sabbath—or an evil one? To preserve life—or to destroy it?" At this they remained silent. 5 He looked around at them with anger, for he was deeply grieved that they had closed their minds against him. Then he said to the man, "Stretch out your hand." The man did so and his hand was perfectly restored. 6 When the Pharisees went outside, they immediately began to plot with the Herodians how they might destroy him.

Discussion Article: Who Is Jesus?

In Mark's gospel, Jesus breaks onto the stage of history, his way prepared by the Baptist's resounding cry in the wilderness: "One more powerful than I is to come after me. I am not fit to stoop and untie His sandal straps. I have baptized you with water; He will baptize you with the Holy Spirit" (1:7–8).

Who is this Jesus, this more powerful One, who will baptize with the Holy Spirit? These identity questions are pivotal to the message of Mark and crucial to the proper engagement of the reader in the journey of faith that the gospel envisions. The gospels are faith proclamations—not mere biographies—and as such, they aim to elicit a faith response from the reader. For Mark, the faith response becomes an incarnation of trust, the fruit of a deep personal relationship. The central question of faith is: In whom do I trust? not: What do I believe?

At the turning point of Mark's gospel, just as at the turning point of our lives, Jesus asks his would-be disciples two critical questions concerning his identity: "Who do people say that I am?" and, more importantly, "And *you,* who do *you* say that I am?" (8:27,29). Like Peter, we must be able to answer personally. It is not enough to recite time-honored confessions, nor merely to mouth popular piety (8:27,28). Jesus wants more than "lip service" and "empty reverence" (7:6). He searches our hearts for the childlike trust in his guidance that will enable us to journey with him to the fulfillment of the Christian mission—a way that leads to the life-giving sacrifice of the Cross.

An authentic response to the question: Who is Jesus? sets in motion a process of conversion that becomes a journey of faith and discipleship. The keener and truer our perception of Jesus' identity, the more radical our following him becomes. As we allow ourselves to be drawn further into the mystery of his person, our understanding and responsibility deepen proportionately. Discipleship becomes an imperative of faith; as a result, we take the pattern of Jesus' life and death as our own. We learn that Jesus' way leads to the Cross, but that, contrary to expectation, the Cross represents not defeat and destruction, but victory and healing. This gospel paradox, namely, that the way to preserve one's life is to lose it for the sake of Christ and the gospel (8:35), stands as the touchstone of true Christian fidelity.

The journey of faith begins at the Lord's invitation; he finds us in our places of marginal existence—in our personal Galilees—where we hunger for good news and the promise of liberation. There, the Lord announces a healing proclamation: "This is the time of fulfillment! The reign of God is at hand! Reform your lives and believe in the gospel" (1:15). Our lives, our ways of seeing, judging and acting are transformed by Christ as we experience his reign in our midst. We need to give ourselves over to the process of conversion and to be taught the path of discipleship. We are called to journey from the place of initial encounter with the life-giving words and healing touch of Christ to the fullness of communion with his life and mission, Cross and resurrection. As disciples, we trace Christ's steps from the marginal places where hope first ignites, through the deepening of faith, to the test of love. Following Jesus, we gradually come to appreciate that the journey of discipleship leads inexorably to the Cross and beyond the empty tomb to fuller life and renewed mission.

CONFLICT OF AUTHORITIES: DIVINE OR HUMAN

For contemporary believers, the *authority* of Jesus rests on his *identity* as the Christ and the Son of God, and indeed, it is with just these titles that Mark introduces Jesus (1:1). For the first disciples, however, the opposite was true, they came to know Jesus' *identity* by first experiencing his *authority*.

Mark records the earliest reaction to Jesus thus: "The people were spellbound by his teaching because he taught with authority and not like the scribes . . . All who looked on were amazed. They began to ask one another: What does this mean? A completely new teaching in a spirit of authority. He gives orders to unclean spirits and they obey him!" (1:22,27). From the beginning people sense a power and authority in Jesus they had not known before in their religious leaders. Jesus is different. His words authoritatively proclaim "a completely new teaching," and his actions convey the divine energies of mercy and compassion. People begin to wonder deeply: Who is this Jesus?

For each person in the gospel who responds to the revelation of Jesus' identity with awe and expectancy, another recoils with indignation at the presumption of his claims. To some, Jesus is the longed-for liberator; to others, he is a rank blasphemer and an insidious threat to orthodoxy. In either case, Jesus demands attention. One's perception of Jesus determines the nature of one's response, lines of allegiance and enmity form early, and intensify with time. Mark carefully charts peoples' various perceptions of Jesus and their diverse reactions to him. We, reading the gospel today, respond to Jesus with the same diversity, and so it becomes our story as well. We are invited to enter into the Spirit's dynamic which calls disciples in every age. The critical issues then become: What is my perception of Jesus? and What will be my response?

As early as chapter 2, the radical nature of Christ's claims begin to make their impact, and consequently, his authority is challenged by the guardians of the status quo. After sketching a typical day in the life of Jesus, Mark presents five rapid scenes depicting him in conflict with various opponents (2:1–3:6). Jesus' authority becomes the critical focus of each incident; each time his opponents ask more stridently: Why does he act in this way, what gives him the *right* to "violate" sacred traditions and ancient religious practices? These questions put to any other person would be legitimate, but because they are put to Jesus, there can be no satisfactory answer unless the questioner possesses a receptive faith. Jesus, as the decisive agent of God's kingdom, is the Lord who rightly determines what is sacred or profane.

All five conflicts by their imagery and content enrich our understanding of Jesus' identity, and at the same time, disclose God's plan of salvation in Christ. In each incident, Jesus reveals divine values and priorities by word and deed. Conflict occurs when these divine standards—namely, mercy and compassion—clash with the stone-cold dictates of tradition or self-righteous piety. Jesus offers sinners fullness of life and divine intimacy, and his opponents resent him for it. Jesus requires conversion from his followers, but these opponents stand arrogantly secure in their knowledge of the law and the prophets. Their self-righteousness blinds them to Jesus and to the limitless compassion of the God he mediates. They refuse to abandon their constricting notions of God; with their paralyzed faith and withered love, they become countersigns to the healing Jesus has come to offer. The humble, the receptive, the broken are healed physically and spiritually, while the proud and the complacent harden their hearts and close their minds (3:5). The contrast of responses is instructive for all disciples.

THE PARALYTIC AND THE MAN WITH THE WITHERED HAND

The arrival of the paralytic carried to Jesus by his friends serves as the occasion for Christ to address a more crippling malady, the paralysis of spirit that arises out of sin and hardness of heart. Heedless of public ridicule and censure, four faith-filled friends of a paralyzed man tear open the roof over Jesus in order to lower their companion into his presence. Such faith and childlike trustfulness cannot go unrewarded; it is just this suppleness of spirit that Jesus is looking for and works wonders with. Jesus forgives the man his sins!

We may be disappointed with this solution to the man's dilemma. We wonder why at first Jesus seems *only* to forgive the man his sins, and does not cure his paralysis. At the same time we read that the scribes in Jesus' audience are horrified at his presumption. They deem it blasphemy on Jesus' part that he claims to exercise the *divine* prerogative to forgive sins. For us, the physical cure is the most miraculous outcome, but for the scribes, the spiritual healing proposed is utterly fantastic and, in fact, not to be believed. The vital connection between these two works of power—forgiving and healing—illuminates the story and provides its lasting significance.

In Jesus' day every spiritual and bodily infirmity was viewed as a consequence of sin. Sickness, paralysis, blindness, leprosy, demonic possession—all proceeded from the same root cause, personal or inherited sinfulness. Therefore, in the people's minds, every time Jesus healed, forgave sins, or expelled unclean spirits it was a sign that God was at work rolling back the dominion of sin and death and establishing in its place the reign of divine life and mercy. All of Christ's healing, reconciling acts—both in his early ministry and in his mission's climax on the Cross—were signs of God's promised victory over sin and death. Each healing gave substance to Christ's claim that the time of fulfillment and the decisive reign of God were at hand! Jesus, as healer and forgiver of sins, showed himself to be the agent of God's victory.

Jesus' action in this gospel incident is decisive. He goes right to the heart of the problem—the release of the spiritual bondage of which the physical paralysis is only a sign. In each of the five conflicts in this section of Mark's gospel, Jesus holds out the promise of fuller life. He resists those things that stunt or maim human life—paralyzed bodies, sinful lives, narrow judgments, lifeless religious practices, unconverted hearts, and closed minds. Jesus stands for compassion, reconciliation, healing, and divine intimacy. These are God's priorities; any human standards to the contrary must undergo conversion.

Sadly, by the end of the fifth conflict it seems that the paralysis Jesus sought to dispel in the first incident has reappeared to claim new victims. This time the spiritual immobility is clearly in evidence, not hidden under the guise of physical infirmity. And this time, the paralyzed—the Pharisees—stiffen at the far-reaching mercy of Jesus and thoroughly resist his healing touch. Their behavior emerges as a cynical parody of the trusting foursome who brought their friend to Jesus. The Pharisees "kept an eye on Jesus to see whether he would heal on the sabbath, hoping to be able to bring an accusation against him" (3:2).

Jesus challenges these so-called religious leaders to exercise their teaching office wisely by distilling the essence of the sabbath law observance. "He said to them: 'Is it permitted to do a good deed on the sabbath—or an evil one? To preserve life—or to destroy it?' " (3:4). Jesus argues that the purpose of the sabbath is to promote life and the good of people; how then can a rigid interpretation of the law that denies life and health, be consistent with the divine intention. Their stony silence angers Christ; he is "deeply grieved that they (have) closed their minds against him" (3:5). There will be no healing for them, not because Jesus does not offer it, but because their sullen self-righteousness puts a barrier between them and God's compassion.

People such as these are the only hopeless cases. Refusing to admit their woundedness, they proudly rebuff the Healer's approach, preferring instead to masquerade as fit and strong.

THE PROMISE OF LIFE

The two healing stories show Christ in opposition to the narrow limits certain people would place on the compassion of God, while the three intervening stories graphically convey the full life and divine intimacy Jesus offers to those who follow him. Despite their ancient origin and long tradition, those human values and customs that block the compassionate love and mercy of God no longer apply. Whatever subverts human life must submit to the judgment of Christ. Jesus is the powerful "Son of Man (who) has authority on earth to forgive sins" (2:10). He alone can accomplish the cosmic healing that is the reconciliation of the human and the divine.

The three central confrontations involve incidents where Jesus is eating with his disciples. This meal context is highly significant, for meals symbolize intimacy and communion. People do not ordinarily break the bread of their lives with just anyone! Meals are celebrations of bondedness and kinship. At a meal the very substance of life is shared, and those who partake become sharers of a common life. Both Jesus and his questioners are keenly aware of this implication.

When Jesus dines with Levi, the tax-collector-turned-disciple, and his outcast friends, some scribes of the Pharisee party are scandalized by Christ's implicit communion with sinners. They complain: "Why does He eat with such as these?" (2:16). For them, disdaining the company of sinners is a sign of righteousness. The problem is that all—except Jesus—are sinners! If he followed the scribes' human standard of judgment, Jesus, the "Holy One of God" (1:24), should disdain *their* company as well. But, that is not God's way, the way of limitless compassion and unconditional love. Jesus offers everyone a chance to repent, even these proud officials: "People who are healthy do not need a doctor; sick people do. I have *come to call sinners,* not the self-righteous" (2:17). Jesus' is a ministry of universal healing.

The *full* realization of the healing, reconciling love of God in Christ will be celebrated in the great messianic banquet of salvation to which Jesus invites all sinners. He is to be the groom, the guest of honor, the cause of rejoicing at that wedding feast! He will consummate the marriage of the human and the divine that God has been preparing throughout salvation history. Jesus reveals the union that God desires and becomes himself the bond of that intimacy. This is the Good News that Jesus announces in the third controversy, the apex of Mark's conflict exposition.

Replying to the criticism that his disciples neglect fasting, Jesus declares that since a wedding is in progress, fasting is inappropriate. With the groom's eagerly awaited appearance, the wedding feast of salvation has begun! His coming suspends ordinary activity; new ways of being and behaving are the order of the day. Jesus captures the necessary response of conversion in two concrete images: new wine in old wineskins, and the new patch on an old garment. The mentality that suggests making do with the old—with minor adjustments for the new—is unrealistic and tempts fate. The new wine of the kingdom will burst the old wineskins of religious formalism with its expansive vitality and power. A thorough-going conversion is required; we must become new vessels in order to contain Christ's spirit. Jesus warns of the danger of trying to apply our Christianity as a new patch on our otherwise unredeemed lives. Such efforts will be both futile and destructive. Instead, we must be made new. We must "reform (our) lives and believe in the gospel" (1:15).

By sharing the bread of his presence at a meal with outcast sinners, Jesus celebrates the communion which he—as groom—has come to offer. God and sinners are united in Christ if these sinners recognize the groom's coming and respond by renewing their lives. Some trusted forms of the past, however, have become split and worn, and now impede the overflowing compassion of God. These require renewal or replacement. In the final two conflicts the sabbath becomes just such a challenge.

When chided by the Pharisees for allowing his hungry disciples to pick and eat grain on the sabbath, Jesus draws a parallel between his act of authoritative compassion and that of King David. Using the Pharisees' own brand of scriptural argumentation, Jesus invites his opponents to a faith-filled perception of both the situation at hand and the underlying purpose of the sabbath. Jesus, like the revered King David, knows the ways of God and acts with divine authority. Besides aligning himself with King David—a messianic expectation in itself— Jesus stuns his Pharisaic audience by claiming: "The Son of Man is lord even of the sabbath" (2:28), that is, God himself! The sabbath is the Lord's day, and Jesus asserts his jurisdiction over it by reclaiming its divine intent: "The sabbath was made for man, not man for the sabbath" (2:27). Jesus, the Son of Man, of the line of David, is the messianic mediator of divine standards and authentic means of access to the divine. Jesus is the Way.

"CLEARLY, THIS MAN WAS THE SON OF GOD!"

When Jesus defies the hard-hearted judgment of the Pharisees by curing the man's withered hand, he seals his fate and journeys toward the Cross. We read: "When the Pharisees went outside, they immediately began to plot with the Herodians (their natural enemies!) how they might destroy him" (3:6). The lines of conflict are drawn. Jesus makes his stand for the preservation of life (3:4) and the restoration of people to wholeness. The Cross of Christ represents the fulfillment of his lifelong passion. It is cosmic healing, the reconciliation of the human and the divine. On the Cross, Jesus hangs silently stretched between heaven and earth, a wordless parable of the reign of God overtaking a human heart, utterly transforming its frail capacities for love and sacrifice. The innocent, totally selfless, gift of Christ's life on Calvary so mirrors God's passion for reconciliation that seeing it, a pagan on-looker is moved to acclaim Jesus, "Son of God" (15:39).

Jesus' death on the Cross is both a radical healing and an eloquent teaching. The Cross of Jesus heals the malaise of the human heart: the sick hunger for power and invincibility, the self-righteous exclusivity, the paralysis of trust and the despair of God's promises of deliverance and new life. In place of these, Jesus teaches servanthood, humility, and forgiveness; he exemplifies the risks that open the human to the divine—faith, hope, and love. These totally accessible means of salvation light the way to God for all sinners. We do not need "to be like God"—the original temptation! We need only become like Jesus: loving, forgiving, faithful to our humanity, and consummately trusting in God.

Like Jesus on the Cross our human poverty and powerlessness, embraced and risked in loving fidelity to the plan of God, becomes salvific. God's power blazes forth in human weakness. Thus it is, that in Mark's gospel, the climactic confession of Jesus' identity as Son of God comes at Christ's moment of greatest vulnerability. Fittingly, the testimony is uttered by one of the lowest and most despised, a Gentile and a member of the hated army of occupation. It is to such as these, who know their need of God, that the eyes of faith are given. The centurion who stood guard by Jesus, on seeing the manner of his death, declared, "Clearly, this man was the Son of God!" (15:39).

Discussion Questions

1. There are perhaps as many ideas about who Jesus Christ is as there are Christian believers. Discuss the various ways people think of Jesus from the "Good Shepherd" to the "Superstar." Is there a criterion to be found in Mark's gospel that distinguishes a false conception about Jesus' identity from a true one? How do the disciples perceive him? Who do you say that Jesus Christ is? How has your life experience affected your perception of Jesus?

2. (a) The Pharisees are not evil people, but they are led into an evil conspiracy against Jesus because they experience him as a threat. Discuss the occasions in the gospel reading when Jesus' behavior most outrages them. What does he threaten in their lives?

   (b) Robert Aldridge in his article "The Courage to Start" describes his experience in dealing with a similar challenge posed by his daughter. What are the values that shaped his life at work before his change? What values caused him to change his attitude and job? Identify the places in your life where your security and lifestyle are threatened by the advent of something new and challenging? Are there persons you know who make you uncomfortable because they pose such a threat to you?

3. What do the healing acts of Jesus signify? What is the relationship between Jesus' acts of healing and his forgiving sins? Can you recall an experience in which your forgiving someone else—or even yourself—produced a healing power? How can the gospel dynamic of forgiveness and healing be applied to situations of international conflict?

4. Discuss the article's interpretation of the parables concerning new wine in old wineskins and a new patch on an old garment? What dangers does Jesus warn us about? Give specific examples. How do our habits and accustomed ways of thinking prevent us from being made new? Has your attitude toward war been made new because of your Christian belief?

Closing Reflection: Mark 2:21–22

No one sews a patch of unshrunken cloth on an old cloak. If one should do so, the very thing used to cover the hole would pull away—the new from the old—and the tear would get worse. Similarly, no person pours new wine into old wineskins. If one does so, the wine will burst the skins and both wine and skins will be lost. No, new wine is poured into new skins.

SESSION 2

The Journey
of Discipleship

Opening Prayer

*Dearest Jesus, you ask us to journey with you to the heart of fidelity—
the Cross. Accept our desire to follow you, and help us overcome our
residual fears of following in your path of ultimate service and sacrifice. Like Peter, we long to boldly confess you before our brothers
and sisters in this world, but too often we share his blindness and
resistance to the Cross. Empower us to take risks of faith for your
sake and for the gospel, to risk laying down our lives and our instruments of destruction in the belief that you will not leave us in death,
but raise us to new life. In disarming our hearts of fear, arrogance,
and the need to "lord it over" others, may we come to that trusting
openness which sees you in every child of God and rejoices to welcome you there. In welcoming you in our midst now, may we grow
more like you and learn from you what it means to "take up the Cross
and follow in (your) steps." This we pray in struggle, remembering
your mercy.* Amen.

Gospel Reading: Mark 8:22–38; 9:30–37; 10:32–52
(For a shorter reading: 8:27–38)

8 A BLIND MAN AT BETHSAIDA. ²² When they arrived at Bethsaida,
some people brought him a blind man and begged him to touch him.
²³ Jesus took the blind man's hand and led him outside the village.
Putting spittle on his eyes he laid his hands on him and asked, "Can
you see anything?" ²⁴ The man opened his eyes and said, "I can see
people but they look like walking trees!" ²⁵ Then a second time Jesus
laid hands on his eyes, and he saw perfectly; his sight was restored
and he could see everything clearly. ²⁶ Jesus sent him home with the
admonition, "Do not even go into the village."

THE MESSIAH. [27] Then Jesus and his disciples set out for the villages around Caesarea Philippi. On the way he asked his disciples this question: "Who do people say that I am?" [28] They replied, "Some, John the Baptizer, others, Elijah, still others, one of the prophets." [29] "And you," he went on to ask, "who do you say that I am?" Peter answered him, "You are the Messiah!" [30] Then he gave them strict orders not to tell anyone about him.

FIRST TEACHING: PASSION AND RESURRECTION. [31] He began to teach them that the Son of Man had to suffer much, be rejected by the elders, the chief priests, and the scribes, be put to death, and rise three days later. [32] He said these things quite openly. Peter then took him aside and began to remonstrate with him. [33] At this he turned around and, eyeing the disciples, reprimanded Peter: "Get out of my sight, you satan! You are not judging by God's standards but by man's."

THE DOCTRINE OF THE CROSS. [34] He summoned the crowd with his disciples and said to them: "If a man wishes to come after me, he must deny his very self, take up his cross, and follow in my steps. [35] Whoever would preserve his life will lose it, but whoever loses his life for my sake and the gospel's will preserve it. [36] What profit does a man show who gains the whole world and destroys himself in the process? [37] What can a man offer in exchange for his life? [38] If anyone in this faithless and corrupt age is ashamed of me and my doctrine, the Son of Man will be ashamed of him when he comes with the holy angels in his Father's glory."

9 SECOND TEACHING: PASSION AND RESURRECTION. [30] They left that district and began a journey through Galilee, but he did not want anyone to know about it. [31] He was teaching his disciples in this vein: "The Son of Man is going to be delivered into the hands of men who will put him to death; three days after his death he will rise." [32] Though they failed to understand his words, they were afraid to question him.

AGAINST AMBITION AND ENVY. [33] They returned to Capernaum and Jesus, once inside the house, began to ask them, "What were you discussing on the way home?" [34] At this they fell silent, for on the way they had been arguing about who was the most important. [35] So he sat down and called the Twelve around him and said, "If anyone wishes to rank first, he must remain the last one of all and the servant of all." ³⁶Then he took a little child, stood him in their midst, and putting his arms around him, said to them, ³⁷ "Whoever welcomes a child such as this for my sake welcomes me. And whoever welcomes me welcomes, not me, but him who sent me."

10 THIRD TEACHING: PASSION AND RESURRECTION. ³²The disciples were on the road going up to Jerusalem, with Jesus walking in the lead. Their mood was one of wonderment, while that of those who followed was fear. Taking the Twelve aside once more, he began to tell them what was going to happen to him. ³³ "We are on our way up to Jerusalem, where the Son of Man will be handed over to the chief priests and the scribes. ³⁴They will condemn him to death and hand him over to the Gentiles, who will mock him and spit at him, flog him, and finally kill him. But three days later he will rise."

AMBITION OF JAMES AND JOHN. ³⁵Zebedee's sons, James and John, approached him. "Teacher," they said, "we want you to grant our request." ³⁶ "What is it?" he asked. ³⁷They replied, "See to it that we sit, one at your right and the other at your left, when you come into your glory." ³⁸Jesus told them, "You do not know what you are asking. Can you drink the cup I shall drink or be baptized in the same bath of pain as I?" ³⁹ "We can," they told him. Jesus said in response, "From the cup I drink of you shall drink; the bath I am immersed in you shall share. ⁴⁰But as for sitting at my right or my left, that is not mine to give; it is for those to whom it has been reserved." ⁴¹The other ten, on hearing this, became indignant at James and John. ⁴²Jesus called them together and said to them: "You know how among the Gentiles those who seem to exercise authority lord it over them; their great ones make their importance felt. ⁴³It cannot be like that with you. Anyone among you who aspires to greatness must serve the rest; ⁴⁴whoever wants to rank first among you must serve the needs of all. ⁴⁵The Son of Man has not come to be served but to serve—to give his life in ransom for the many."

THE BLIND BARTIMAEUS. ⁴⁶They came to Jericho next, and as he was leaving that place with his disciples and a sizable crowd, there was a blind beggar Bartimaeus ("son of Timaeus") sitting by the roadside.

[47] On hearing that it was Jesus of Nazareth, he began to call out, "Jesus, Son of David, have pity on me!" [48] Many people were scolding him to make him keep quiet, but he shouted all the louder, "Son of David, have pity on me!" [49] Then Jesus stopped and said, "Call him over." So they called the blind man over, telling him as they did so, "You have nothing to fear from him! Get up! He is calling you!" [50] He threw aside his cloak, jumped up and came to Jesus. [51] Jesus asked him, "What do you want me to do for you?" "Rabboni," the blind man said, "I want to see." [52] Jesus said in reply, "Be on your way! Your faith has healed you." Immediately he received his sight and started to follow him up the road.

Discussion Article: The Journey of Discipleship

Our journey of discipleship begins when we, like Peter at Caesarea Philippi (8:29), confess our belief that Jesus is the Messiah and Lord of life. Upon making this initial confession, the lifelong journey of faith and conversion is inaugurated. For once we perceive who Jesus is, we must then take up his cross and follow in his steps. As disciples, we journey from the fringes of faith—where liberation is bountifully promised—to the heart of faithfulness where liberation is wondrously fulfilled in servanthood, the giving of life for others. Jesus assures us in responding to his call that the path of discipleship will lead to new life.

Mark's journey narrative in chapters eight through ten contains the heart of Christ's instruction on discipleship. On his way from Galilee, the place of the marginalized, to Jerusalem, as the center of Jewish life and worship, Jesus painstakingly teaches the meaning of his life and death. Here in the city that kills the prophets, he equips his followers for the arduous but rewarding path of Gospel fidelity. Three times Jesus predicts his suffering, death, and resurrection, and three times his disciples resist the idea that Jesus the Messiah must also be the Suffering Servant. Each time Jesus patiently teaches his baffled disciples the values of his Kingdom: forgiveness, trust, and unconditional love. As prophet of the Kingdom, Jesus is charged with the vitality of his mission: To proclaim God's reign and to heal the ravages of sin and death. It is in his fundamental commitment to usher in the Kingdom of life that he knowingly accepts the risk of the Cross.

His Cross teaches us that death is vanquished not by a convincing display of divine might but by the power of a humble, forgiving heart surrendered totally to God in love for others. Whenever we open ourselves to the power of the Cross the Kingdom stirs within us. Its power disrupts our lives, challenges our most basic assumptions, and brings us in touch with the root of our being. Our view of the world and of ourselves is transformed. The life of the Kingdom compels us to share, to break down the barriers that separate us, to become vulnerable to the needs of others, and to serve them by walking in the path of the Cross.

For Mark, the journey of discipleship requires a conversion from blindness to sight. The evangelist's account of Jesus' journey to Jerusalem contains not only the basic instruction for true discipleship, but also reveals the blindness and resistance of the disciples to the mission and Cross of Jesus. Mark emphasizes the disciples' spiritual blindness by enclosing the narrative of the three passion predictions with two stories of blind men being healed: the blind man at Bethsaida (8:22–26), and Bartimaeus (10:46–52). It is their utter faith in this stranger Jesus that enables his healing power to be present in them and to affect them. Their blindness and cure stand in relief to the symbolic blindness of the disciples who again and again reject the efficacy of the Cross.

In our age, we too struggle with the problem of blindness, often failing to grasp the significance of Jesus' mission. The very existence of nuclear weapons in our society is a profound manifestation of our own moral and spiritual blindness. Our intention to use these weapons fully contradicts Jesus' teachings and his suffering and death on the Cross. To confront this nuclear intention as people of faith is to expose, confess, and overcome this evil as well as blindness to it.

Like the blind Bethsaidan whose cure takes repeated applications of Christ's healing hands, and like the twelve, who require three passion predictions to open their eyes to the power and wisdom of the Cross, we contemporary disciples need to be continuously touched and taught by Christ. Our efforts to overcome our moral and spiritual blindness and to be sustained by faith in this nuclear age rest on our choice to be touched by Jesus and to follow his way of the Cross.

LESSONS IN DISCIPLESHIP

At the turning point of the gospel when for the first time one of the disciples is able to say of Jesus publicly: "You are the Messiah" (8:29), Jesus seizes the opportunity to instruct his disciples on the *real* meaning of his messiahship. "He began to teach them that the Son of Man had to suffer much, be rejected by the elders, the chief priests, and the scribes, be put to death and rise three days later" (8:31). This prospect appalls Peter. He resists it, takes Jesus aside, and tries to dissuade him from the way of the Cross. Jesus' reaction to Peter's appeal is stunning. "Get out of my sight, you satan! You are not judging by God's standards, but by man's!" (8:33). The vehemence of Christ's words sobers us, and makes us note all the more carefully the source of Jesus' anger: Peter, although he recognizes Jesus as the Messiah, finds it unthinkable that the Christ should have to suffer. By his response, Peter shows himself blind to the healing and saving power that the free gift of one's life for others can achieve. Peter, like all disciples, must be taught *Jesus'* way of salvation, the way of the Kingdom. The disciple is still thinking in the categories of the world; he prefers the path of security and untroubled glory to Christ's way of love and humble servanthood.

A second and a third time, Jesus tries to break through the disciples' blindness in an effort to teach the way that the Kingdom will come— lifegiving sacrifice. Each time, Jesus' prediction of his saving death/resurrection receives scant response. The pathos of a man charged with the vitality of life and love who nonetheless embraces death for the sake of his loved ones is the stuff of great tragedy, yet the disciples seem unmoved and uncomprehending. The paradox of Jesus' messiahship—that God's Son should have to give his life in ransom for theirs—is too much for them, so they lapse into more manageable concerns. On both occasions they begin to argue among themselves about who is greatest. Their ambition for prestige and places of glory is the exact counterpoint of Jesus' self-revelation as Suffering Servant. He promises to give of himself to the point of death, while his followers vie for positions of security and influence.

The teachings Jesus offers each time he promises his own life for the sake of others are difficult for the worldly power-seeking disciples to grasp. Even as they follow him in journey, they close their eyes to the risk of sacrifice, to the risk of the Cross. Jesus patiently teaches that unless we deny ourselves by emptying our hearts of self-centered ambition, and begin to spend ourselves as he did in the service of our brothers and sisters, we cannot call ourselves his followers. However, if we *do* risk losing our lives in servanthood, we are promised that this self-denial will yield ultimate self-fulfillment. We will preserve our lives in the sight of God and assure ourselves of places with Christ in his kingdom. The alternative is grim. If we reject the Cross and seek to preserve our lives by any means other than union with Jesus' path of servanthood, we risk alienation from Christ (8:31) and exile from his kingdom.

In contrast to the disciples' desire to be greatest, Jesus identifies himself with a child, and declares that the quality of our welcome for the smallest and the least is the measure of our welcome for him. Christ depicts himself as the child of the loving God unwelcomed in our midst so long as the weak, the poor, the disenfranchised, and the powerless of this world are despised and neglected. We learn that in welcoming these marginal multitudes, these global Galileans, we gain access not only to Christ, but also to the One who sent him. The living God is touched by our welcoming the poor. Suddenly, servanthood assumes new proportions: no longer is it simply justice or charity, it is consummate worship. Welcoming the least becomes serving the greatest!

Still Jesus' disciples are blind to the transforming power God reveals when humble service is coupled with trusting love. The ways of might and domination prevalent among the powerful of their day tempt them to mistrust lowliness. Jesus counters: "It cannot be like that with you. Anyone who aspires to greatness must serve . . . the needs of all. The Son of Man has come not to be served, but to serve—to give his life in ransom for the many" (10:43–45). Humility, servanthood, and love are the only forces strong enough to break the grip of sin and death. To be the greatest, to be the saving Lord of history, Jesus will take the last place on earth—the place of a condemned man—and there serve the needs of all sinners. Christ's followers too must be prepared to welcome such a status and share such a life.

MORAL BLINDNESS AND THE NUCLEAR INTENTION

The Cross of the Suffering Servant heals our vision and opens our minds and hearts. Like the disciples, however, we often resist Jesus' teaching on servanthood as well as the Cross it implies: we prefer to dominate rather than to serve others. No event in our age more significantly demonstrates our blindness toward Christ's values of unconditional forgiveness and love than the existence of nuclear weapons. We have become morally and spiritually blind to the reality of the evil we have created and continue to justify in the name of our own security.

By their very nature nuclear weapons are genocidal instruments of mass murder and indiscriminate destruction. A single nuclear weapon has the capacity to destroy an entire city of people in a few seconds by blast and fire. Its cancer-causing and genetic consequences would affect all biological life in a wider area virtually forever. Many of the fifty thousand nuclear weapons on earth today *individually* contain a greater destructive power than the combined effect of all of the weapons so far used in human history.

Despite this level of violence, two of the most powerful governments on earth continue to amass three to ten nuclear weapons each day. Their mutually reinforcing nuclear war policies are increasingly aggressive: each side has moved in recent years from justifying plans of massive retaliation against the other to the current strategy of using nuclear weapons in an offensive first strike. As arsenals grow and confrontation intensifies, nuclear war, unimaginable as it is, becomes increasingly probable.

The destructive potential of nuclear war is so vast that we cannot comprehend the extent of the evil we have created and have allowed to rule over us. Our attempts to define, to understand, even to control in some ways this capacity to destroy, do not bring us any closer to the conscientious moment of confessing and resisting the basic evil.

Nuclear weapons derive from a long history of human sinfulness— from the first time brother killed brother. The sin of moral blindness wraps itself around the basic death intention obscuring at its heart the ultimate sin nurtured there: the choice of death over life. To be credible, the threat of using nuclear weapons presupposes the intention of using them. This nuclear intention is morally indefensible because what is wrong to do is wrong to threaten to do. It recommends global suicide as a solution to the problems of competing ideologies and economic interests. This murderous intention completely betrays the intention of the Cross: the willingness of Christ to suffer and die for others so that they might live the fullness of his Kingdom.

The nuclear intention is the central violence of our age to which all violence is linked. The violence of starvation, poverty and despair; the violence against children, women, and the unborn; the violence of racism; the violence of state torture and imprisonment; the violence of the street; and the subtle violence of our affluent life-style are all drawn together and reenacted in the cold, dark nuclear intention.

HEALED VISION AND THE VISION OF HEALING

The stories of blind eyes being opened reveal the power of faith that healing requires, and the power of love that healing becomes. This healing marks the loss of spiritual isolation and remoteness, and the recovery of moral insight: the ability to see things as they are, to gain an orientation guided by the values of the Kingdom rather than by those of the world.

To discern with open, willful eyes the nuclear intention that we hold within us is to confess our own complicity in the central violence of our age. To behold this evil perpetuated throughout human history and contaminating the human spirit is to ask God to forgive us for something we fear is too terrible to forgive, too large and complex for us to undo even with God's help. But when we are touched by the healing power of the Cross we see ourselves revealed as both nuclear victim and sinner, although we do not want to be either. Our blindness to the reality of nuclear weapons and to our responsibility for them enables us to hide this terrible sin, thus compounding it. Like Peter, we ask Christ to be reasonable, to be reconciled with the worldly values even though they have produced in our time the means to destroy every living thing on earth.

True sight comes gradually for us, as it did for the nameless Bethsaidan. Jesus patiently asks us again and again: "Can you see anything?" Somehow our blindness has heightened our sense of touch: we recognize in the strong though gentle hands of Christ a healing power that we know can transform our vision and our lives. There is an unexpected intimacy to the feel of these crucified hands. His touch penetrates the scars left from past wounds, exposes and opens our hearts, and enables us to risk vulnerable love. By inviting the hands of Christ to cover our face, we confess the spiritual blindness that afflicts us personally and as a society, and we dare to ask for eyes of faith that will see through the false values we had embraced. The risk of confession, of repentance, becomes the invitation to wholeness, to healing. It is the risk of the Cross.

To overcome blindness we must be prepared to journey to be healed, and then to journey further once healed. The journey is both the test and consequence of faith. It can lead us through unfamiliar terrain, even to Jerusalem and the Cross. Yet Christ's healing touch impels a journey filled with a longing for the Kingdom. We move

away from the sick place of our hearts in following the One whose act
of heart—the Cross—transforms us. Our eyes of faith perceive this
Cross of Jesus as the instrument of healing and new life for all.

Discussion Questions

1. (a) Is the Cross a frightening symbol for you? How does it
    change in meaning when it is linked with the resurrection (as Je-
    sus links them in his three passion predictions)? How is it possible
    to think of the Cross as a symbol of life and healing? What are
    the everyday ways people experience the Cross and resurrection?

    (b) Jesus was not one to allow himself to be manipulated, yet he
    seemed to allow himself to be victimized by the powers of the
    world. How do you account for this apparent contradiction? What
    does Christ's death and resurrection teach us about the nature of
    power—the power of the world and the power of the Kingdom?
    Which power was more real to the disciples? Which is more real
    to you? Is the Cross a symbol of power or powerlessness—or
    both? Is the worldly notion of peace through military strength
    compatible with the way of the Cross?

2. To be a servant is a lowly status according to the standards of the
    world. Why is there special dignity in the servanthood to which
    the gospel calls us? What power is being served? What practical
    results does this service hope to achieve? Why must the servant
    be prepared to suffer? What concrete examples do you know of in
    which someone's willing self-sacrifice has promoted the life of
    another?

3. (a) Throughout human history threats of violence have contin-
    ually been carried out—war is a constant human experience. Do
    you believe that the threat to use nuclear weapons is rooted in the
    full intention to use them? Is this intention merely a feature of
    international policy or does it stem more deeply from the human
    heart? Can you identify this intention as being yours personally?
    If so, how can you struggle to remove it? What does this intention
    have to do with power? What does it have to do with the Cross?

    (b) Do you believe, as the article suggests, that the nuclear inten-
    tion is morally connected to every act of violence in our culture?

Discuss the ways in which the violence of nuclear weapons is related to the violence we see in our society.

4. What do we learn from the contrast between the blind men who were healed and the twelve who persistently resisted Christ's teaching about his messiahship? What blinded the disciples to the way of the cross and Jesus' role as Suffering Servant? Are we as struggling disciples of Christ today also blind in similar ways? In what ways does our nuclear intention reveal us as morally and spiritually blind? Why is it so difficult to *want* to see? What risks must we be willing to take so that we may be healed of this blindness? What can we learn from the action of Bartimaeus and the Bethsaidan?

Closing Reflection: Mark 8:34–36

Jesus summoned the crowd with his disciples and said to them: If you wish to come after me, you must deny your very self, take up your cross, and follow in my steps. Whoever would preserve one's life will lose it, but whoever loses one's life for my sake and the gospel's will preserve it. What profit does a person show who gains the whole world but is destroyed in the process?

To Trust In
God's Promise

Opening Prayer

Loving God, we have broken so many promises we made to you. Yet you keep your promises to us. Enable us to recognize more clearly and fully the power of the promise you make, the promise of Jesus to heal us, the promise of the Spirit who stirs in our hearts. We pray that we may see your word as a promise for each day, each moment, each experience. Help us, dear God, to renounce the false promises we make to ourselves, the false gods we create in our midst when we dare to doubt your promise. Increase in us a trust in the promise of life that you bring, not in the promise of death that we in our failure depend upon. Help us to become more trustful and forgiving of others—and of ourselves—more prayerful in all that we do. We ask this in the name of Jesus, your Son, who trusts us more than we know. Amen.

Gospel Reading: Mark 11:11–25

11 He entered Jerusalem and went into the temple precincts. He inspected everything there, but since it was already late in the afternoon, he went out to Bethany accompanied by the Twelve.

JESUS CURSES A FIG TREE. ¹² The next day when they were leaving Bethany he felt hungry. ¹³ Observing a fig tree some distance off, covered with foliage, he went over to see if he could find anything on it. When he reached it he found nothing but leaves; it was not the time for figs. ¹⁴ Then addressing it he said, "Never again shall anyone eat of your fruit!" His disciples heard all this.

CLEANSING OF THE TEMPLE. ¹⁵ When they reached Jerusalem, Jesus entered the temple precincts and began to drive out those who were engaged in buying and selling. He overturned the money-changers' tables and the stalls of the men selling doves; [16] moreover, he would not permit anyone to carry things through the temple area.

[17] Then he began to teach them: "Does not Scripture have it, 'My house shall be called a house of prayer for all peoples'— ? but you have turned it into a den of thieves." [18] The chief priests and the scribes heard of this and began to look for a way to destroy him. They were at the same time afraid of him because the whole crowd was under the spell of his teaching. [19] When evening drew on, Jesus and his disciples went out of the city. [20] Early next morning, as they were walking along, they saw the fig tree withered to its roots. [21] Peter remembered and said to him, "Rabbi, look! The fig tree you cursed has withered up." [22] In reply Jesus told them: "Put your trust in God. [23] I solemnly assure you, whoever says to this mountain, 'Be lifted up and thrown into the sea,' and has no inner doubts but believes that what he says will happen, shall have it done for him. [24] I give you my word, if you are ready to believe that you will receive whatever you ask for in prayer, it shall be done for you. [25] When you stand to pray, forgive anyone against whom you have a grievance so that your heavenly Father may in turn forgive you your faults."

Discussion Article: To Trust in God's Promise

The demonstration of holy anger in the temple marks the high point of Jesus' confrontation with the religious authorities of his day. This *action* of cleansing the temple contrasts dramatically with the course of events it precipitates, the *passion* of the Cross. This contrast of a disruptive Jesus in the temple and a suffering Jesus on the Cross accentuates the judgment that he offers in both moments. His is a judgment and a call to the people in the tradition of the prophets of Israel to return to the way of God.

Jesus' indignation toward the empty formalism of the temple is prefigured in the story in which he curses the fig tree. In juxtaposing these stories Mark interprets both the wrath of Jesus and the hypocrisy of the temple that it reveals. The tree symbolically illustrates the organic quality of the temple as institution. It is the house of worship with a living tradition, whose roots are watered in the promise of the messiah, a promise ever renewed. The tree is special in Jesus' view— he notices it in the distance and goes out of the way to examine it. He searches the tree for a sign of early fruit, a sign and promise of the fullness of summer to come. But the tree yields no early fruit, just foliage. Jesus does not curse the tree for its frailty or lack of form—

this tree is mature and covered with leaves—but rather for its lack of fruit, its lack of achievement.

THE CLEANSING OF THE TEMPLE

The temple stands fruitless before the Jesus who inspects everything in its precincts upon entering Jerusalem (11:11). No fruitful worship, no sign of an authentic messianic expectation is evident. The prayer and ritual sacrifice of the temple are revealed to be merely gesture and form devoid of an inner faith. In prophetic rage Jesus throws aside the tables of the merchants and money-changers whose business profanes the temple. The same hands that opened blind eyes send the wood crashing to the stone.

Jesus' disruption of temple commerce is meant to clean away all that defiles the temple and subverts true worship. In its abuses temple worship deadens the spirit of the covenant it claims through tradition. Its cleansing represents Jesus' attempt to reclaim the house of God to true prayer by exposing the hypocrisy and spiritual blindness of external religious practices that have no spiritual content.

Jesus' anger reflects as well his response to the injustices caused by the arrangement of temple power: the social privilege, the system of domination that puts the religious authorities above others as a temple class. Jesus' demonstration occurs in the outer court of the Gentiles, the large margin of space that surrounds the priestly sanctuary of prayer and ritual sacrifice. The cleansing thus becomes a demand both for true worship and for justice—justice for the marginal, for the unchosen Gentiles, for the outcasts of Galilee, whose holy space is given over to the worldly interests of the privileged. Jesus cites the prophet Isaiah: "My house shall be called a house of prayer for all peoples" (11:17). The cleansing of the temple follows the call of divine obedience and becomes, at the same time, a radical call for human justice.

"On what authority are you doing these things? Who has given you the power to do them?" (11:28) This is the question with which the religious authorities accuse the angry Christ of the temple. For Christ, the temple cleansing directs the very question of authority to the defenders of empty orthodoxy. On what authority is religious expression emptied of faith? On what authority are the injustices of poverty and inequality tolerated? In proclaiming God's singular authority Jesus challenges us to remove everything that stands in the way of the Kingdom.

NUCLEAR TRUST

On what authority—divine or human—do we rely on nuclear weap
ons for our freedom and security? How can we reconcile our nuclear
trust, our faith in the threat of total death, with our trust in a merciful
God?

Any trust that we put in nuclear weapons is trust displaced from
God and the Kingdom. Our nuclear trust contradicts divine trust. Our
dependence upon the nuclear threat to maintain our own personal and
national security represents in itself our most profound doubt in the
power of God to heal and free us. Since we trust more in the power
of fear and death than we do in the power of forgiveness and life,
destruction is the means we seek and the outcome we have come to
expect. The nuclear plot is a statement of utter despair, of divine mistrust, of radical doubt in the promise of God and in the healing power
of the Cross.

Our trust in nuclear weapons conceals a false, messianic promise—
liberation and security by death-dealing. The bomb becomes a substitute god, an idol to which godlike authority is assigned. We surround
it with an atmosphere of mystery, reverence, and finality. We blindly
trust in these weapons to save us, refusing to see instead that they
promise only annihilation. We forget God's intention for the world
and violate it by nurturing the death intention in our hearts.

Our nuclear trust is an abomination to the holy, an expression of
our faithlessness as a people. It constitutes idolatry. If our nuclear
trust is meant to safeguard our freedom to express our faith in Christ,
then there *is no* true faith—there is only the temple profaned

The activity of the world reflects the activity of our hearts. Our
weak and broken human hearts invite this blind violence to take root
within them, but there is no yield of fruit, only the withering of our
spirits. Insofar as we, a religious people, have supported in our hearts
and in the structures of society this threat of thorough obliteration, we
ourselves have built and sustained an unclean temple. This nuclear
temple of our day begs a raging, cleansing Christ.

IN WHOM DO WE TRUST?

The struggle of the disciples to overcome their blindness to the
meaning of Christ's messianic suffering resembles the problem of discipleship in the nuclear age. Our task is first to discern the messianic
qualities with which we have endowed the technology of self-destruc-

tion, and then to renounce this false worship by turning to and trusting God.

Jesus comforts us with the simple words: "Fear is useless. What is needed is trust" (5:36). This advice speaks to our blindness of heart, and invites us to confess and renounce the nuclear intention that we hide there. Jesus, who brings the gift of life, assures us that God can be trusted, and that "all things are possible" in a trusting relationship with God (10:27).

The morning after the temple cleansing, Jesus and his disciples pass the fig tree he had cursed now withered to its roots. Responding to their amazement he instructs them on the merits of trustfulness and prayer. "Put your trust in God . . . I give you my word, if you are ready to believe that you will receive whatever you ask for in prayer, it shall be done for you. When you stand to pray, forgive anyone against whom you have a grievance so that your heavenly Father may in turn forgive you your faults" (11:22, 24–25).

Jesus calls us to the simple but complete trustfulness of a child. He reminds us that faithfulness consists in expecting and accepting gifts from God, and in seeing others as gifts and becoming a gift to them. Our nuclear trust relationship violates this gift quality of a life of faith. We trust in the threat of death, not in the promise of life. Our death trust kills the vital expectation of gift from the "God of the living" (12:27).

Expectation is the fruit of trustfulness and prayer; it ripens in the form of vigilance. "Learn a lesson from the fig tree," Jesus teaches. "Once the sap of its branches runs high and it begins to sprout leaves, you know that summer is near" (13:28). In fruitful faith we must await God's promise to return, and come to see the interim promise of gifts fulfilled. In nurturing the seeds of our faith, we ourselves become the gift of God. Jesus, the Expected One, urges us to be "constantly on the watch," to have eyes of faith, to avoid dead vision (13:33–34). Watchfulness is the response to Christ's gift of open eyes.

Implicit in the trustful expectancy of prayer is the willingness to forgive others their wrongs, and perhaps more deeply, to forgive ourselves for the wrong of a misplaced trust. Honest prayer and true justice, Christ's motives for cleansing the temple of our hearts, are based on these aspects of inner and outer forgiveness.

The trust and forgiveness to which Jesus calls us radically subverts our dependency upon nuclear weapons. Our trust in God cannot admit a vengeful trust in death-dealing; our forgiveness of brothers and sisters precludes the choice of nuclear murder.

In the new relationship that he offers and becomes, Jesus promises us that prayer can realize a genuine freedom and peace. He insists that forgiveness conditions prayer, that the forgiveness of others secures our own forgiveness before God. Our relationship to God is inseparable from our relationship to one another. This mutuality of relationships—to God and to neighbor—reflects the integration of divine and human aspects in Jesus' own identity and in his passion and action of the Cross. In the shadow of the Cross, he teaches the great but simple commandment of love—the mutual aspects of love that true faithfulness enables.

A scribe approaches Jesus with the question: "Which is the first of all commandments?" Jesus replies: "This is the first: 'Hear, O Israel! The Lord our God is Lord alone! Therefore you shall love the Lord your God with all your heart, with all your soul, with all your mind, and with all your strength.' This is the second: 'You shall love your neighbor as yourself.' There is no other commandment greater than these" (12:29–31). "Excellent Teacher!" the scribe remarks, such love of God and neighbor is "worth more than any burnt offering or sacrifice" (12:33). The scribe perceives the wisdom of Jesus' words. No sacrifice, no temple cult, can replace the virtue of true worship and justice, the love of God and of each person. This commandment unites the divine trust and the human forgiveness that Christ imparts and invites.

Discussion Questions

1. Does Jesus' behavior in cleansing the temple seem uncharacteristic to you? How are his actions there consistent with his role as Suffering Servant? Do you think people watching Jesus were positively or negatively affected? Who were those positively affected? Who negatively affected? What does this suggest about the nature of the kingdom? Can you imagine Christians today acting in a similarly disruptive fashion in pursuing the goals of the kingdom?

2. (a) Everyone is tempted to idol worship, even Christians. What is idolatry? What are the idols that are most often worshiped in our society? Why are they so attractive? In what way is the nu-

clear arms race an expression of our idol worship? Who are the sacrificial victims? Who are the beneficiaries? How do such sacrifices performed by the servants of the powers of death differ in their results from the sacrifices of the servants of the kingdom?

(b) Whom do we trust? Where do we ultimately find our security? What kind of trust does our nuclear arms policies reflect? Is this trust consistent with the gospel message of the kingdom? How do the statements in Appendix 3 attempt to answer these questions? Discuss the statements that struck you the most either because you agree or disagree with them.

3. Discuss some threatening situations you experience in everyday life. What feelings do you experience when threatened? How do you imagine the feelings your aggressor has toward you? What are some Christian ways of dealing with these feelings? Do you think such interpersonal solutions have parallels on an international level? What are the similarities and differences? In light of these considerations, do you think that the Christian pacifist stance in a world of nuclear weapons is naive and impractical? What is ultimately at stake for the pacifist? What is at stake in the variety of other non-pacifist attitudes?

4. When we pray about particular things, prayer more often changes us and our relationship to them than the things themselves. When we pray for world peace, therefore, we pray largely about changing ourselves. What are the concrete changes we hope for when we pray for peace?

Closing Reflection: Mark 11:24–25

I give you my word, if you are ready to believe that you will receive whatever you ask for in prayer, it shall be done for you. When you stand to pray, forgive anyone against whom you have a grievance so that your heavenly Father may in turn forgive you your faults.

SESSION 4

To Risk Eucharistic Love

Opening Prayer

Lord Jesus, without seeing you, we believe that you have come to us in the sign of your body broken, your blood poured out. We hold before you, Lord, this world we live in, a world for which we share responsibility with so many sisters and brothers. Today our world is plagued by weapons of destruction that threaten to annihilate all life God has created. Under the earth, in the oceans, above our heads in planes, tens of thousands of nuclear weapons betray our lack of faithfulness in your eucharistic love and in the gospel call to be peacemakers.

What do you think, Lord, as you look at what we are doing? Jesus, we hear you say that if the human family is to survive we will have to take a position for God's family. We will have to measure what we have, and what our country has, against those who are victims of starvation and gross neglect. We will have to lay down our fear of the "enemy" for, through you, all people are members of the one body. We will have to renounce the nuclear intention in our hearts and strive to break open the blessed bread of our lives and share it with others.

Jesus, help us to turn from our blindness and to risk accepting the gift of your Eucharist. Deepen our trust in your guidance, and give us the strength to witness to your Cross. Enable us to be visible signs of your eucharistic love in this nuclear age. As we seek to be your faithful followers, empower us to give our lives—as you did—in love and service. All glory and praise be to you, Lord Jesus, bread of everlasting life, now and forever. Amen.

Gospel Reading: Mark 14:17–31

14 THE BETRAYER. [17] As it grew dark he arrived with the Twelve [18] They reclined at table, and in the course of the meal Jesus said, "I give you my word, one of you is about to betray me, yes, one who is eating with me." [19]They began to say to him sorrowfully, one by one, "Surely not I!" [20]He said, "It is one of the Twelve—a man who dips into the dish with me. [21]The Son of Man is going the way the Scripture tells of him. Still, accursed be that man by whom the Son of Man is betrayed. It were better for him had he never been born."

THE HOLY EUCHARIST. [22]During the meal he took bread, blessed and broke it, and gave it to them. "Take this," he said, "this is my body." [23]He likewise took a cup, gave thanks and passed it to them, and they all drank from it. [24]He said to them: "This is my blood, the blood of the covenant, to be poured out on behalf of many. [25]I solemnly assure you, I will never again drink of the fruit of the vine until the day when I drink it new in the reign of God."

[26]After singing songs of praise, they walked out to the Mount of Olives.

PETER'S DENIAL FORETOLD. [27]Jesus then said to them: "Your faith in me shall be shaken, for Scripture has it, 'I will strike the shepherd and the sheep will be dispersed.' [28]But after I am raised up, I will go to Galilee ahead of you." [29]Peter said to him, "Even though all are shaken in faith, it will not be that way with me." [30]Jesus answered, "I give you my assurance, this very night before the cock crows twice, you will deny me three times." [31]But Peter kept reasserting vehemently, "Even if I have to die with you, I will not deny you." They all said the same.

Discussion Article: To Risk Eucharistic Love

In the eucharistic bread and wine Jesus offers us the signs of his body and blood. These simple elements of the human meal convey a deep sense of intimacy: this food is offered as a personal gift, to be taken to the most interior part of our being. The Eucharist is food that endures—a gift of love that continually renews our heart.

The Eucharist conveys a love we cannot contain, a love that overwhelms our hearts and our ability to understand it. Not to express this love in turn to one another, even in our often slow and fragile ways, is to renounce it. God places on us, in receiving this love, the demand that we share it with others, especially those, like us, who need this love. The fundamental character of love is that it be given to others in order to receive it fully. This is central to Jesus' teachings on servant-hood and the healing Cross. In this way, the Eucharist and the Cross are related healing moments.

There is a confessional aspect to our sharing in this banquet: we confess our unworthiness to be present at the table. We know the unique brokenness hidden within us. Yet with trust in the Healer we carry it openly to the table as we take our place there in celebration. The Eucharist is a meal for sinners, not the self-righteous. Jesus comes to fill the hungry, not the fed; to heal the sick, not those who are well (2:17). It is the poor, the broken in body and spirit who follow him, who are drawn to the Healer and Teacher. He welcomes them—us—and transforms our poverty to wholeness.

THE EUCHARIST IN THE MIDST OF BETRAYAL AND DENIAL

When we recognize the predictions of betrayal and denial that surround this holy meal, we become aware how immense and resilient is Jesus' love. On the evening that he is betrayed by Judas, denied by Peter and abandoned by the rest, Jesus nonetheless offers them the bread and wine of Eucharist, symbols of his life poured out in love.

Jesus begins this sacred liturgy of self-sacrifice by telling his disciples, "One of you is about to betray me, yes, one who is eating with me—accursed be that man" (14:18). Without hesitation, the disciples sorrowfully respond to Jesus, one by one, saying "Surely not I" (14:19). As on the journey to Jerusalem, the disciples are determined to remain true to their Lord. Yet deep down, in the recesses of their hearts, they still resist the "cup of suffering" that Jesus calls them to. They still cannot accept the Cross as the way to wholeness and new life. While out of failure to recognize their weakness and their impending trial, the disciples say "Surely not I"—we will always remain loyal—the actual test of faith results in their rejection and abandonment of Jesus.

Just as the disciples strive to be faithful to Jesus and then lose faith in times of trial, we contemporary Christians are also prone to failures in fidelity. During moments when we assume we are in control, we can testify that no matter what situation arises, we will remain faithful. Yet when we are directly in the midst of crisis and tension, we give way to fear, and worry about our status and security. We substitute the human values of expediency and self-interest for the divine values of patience and unconditional love.

In contrast, Jesus with foreknowledge that he will be betrayed and denied by his disciples, still offers them his body and blood. By becoming human and identifying with the suffering and marginalized of Galilee, Jesus knows the human condition. He knows that we fail in faith, and need forgiveness and understanding. In expressing the patient, untiring love he has for us, the gift of the Eucharist becomes the ultimate expression of Jesus' love and forgiveness. Amidst his disciples' failure of faith and resistance to the Cross—then and now—Jesus extends with open hands this life-giving bread and saving cup.

"CAN YOU DRINK THE CUP?"

Jesus offers us his all-embracing love in the Eucharist and awaits our response. Can we accept this unconditional love? Are we willing to give our love freely to others in the way which Jesus exemplifies? Can we drink from the cup of suffering that Jesus must drink, so that with him we can be transformed to new life? (10:39).

At the eucharistic meal, Jesus prepares himself as well as his disciples for the road to Calvary. He reveals the imminent suffering and death he would endure by sharing with them crushed wheat and grapes. In lifting up these simple earthly elements, he anticipates his being crushed to become the blood of a new Passover covenant. The covenant he now begins will be completed in the messianic banquet of salvation. Jesus assures us of the salvation he will gain: "Never again will I drink of the fruit of the vine until I drink it new in the reign of God" (14:22–24).

In offering the Eucharist to his disciples on this holy Feast of Unleavened Bread, Jesus reenacts the Passover story. The Passover meal recalls the exodus of the people of Israel from Egypt, the land of slavery. It commemorates God's deliverance of the Hebrew people from the chains of ruthless oppression and recounts their journey of faith to the promised land. Jesus inaugurates a new Passover through the sharing of Eucharist in the shadow of the Cross. For by his death on the Cross all people are delivered from the bondage of sin and death and are offered access to the promised land of salvation. Thus, the last supper reveals to us that Jesus is the deliverer of the new Passover.

For Christians, to receive this new Passover meal is to accept the Cross that is our means of liberation. Our taking the cup means that we, like Jesus, must be willing to be servants of one another and to embrace the great commandment of love. We must be willing to make the sacrifice God requires of us. We must be able to recognize with Jesus that it is through totally giving our lives to serve God and one another that we can be made new people. This total abandonment of self led Jesus to the Cross. Whenever we partake in the Eucharist then, Jesus asks us if we can drink the cup of suffering that he drinks and journey with him to the Cross.

LIVING THE EUCHARIST

The sacred meal of the Eucharist gives us the strength and nourishment we need to confront and be healed of the evils within us and around us. In our day, as we seek to embody the love Jesus gives to us in the Eucharist and to be converted to the way of his Cross, we are faced with great challenges. What does it mean to participate in the Eucharist with a nuclear intention in our hearts and our missiles aimed at our sisters and brothers? Can our nuclear intention be reconciled with the communion that this Eucharist celebrates?

The nuclear intention embodies fear, not love. This intention clearly rejects the love Jesus extends to us in the eucharistic meal. It directly contradicts the healing spirit that the Eucharist seeks to foster. If, as Christians, we truly accept the Eucharist and Cross of Jesus, how can we possibly condone, much less contemplate, the premeditated mass murder of sisters and brothers in Christ! The threat of nuclear murder defiles the Eucharist and rejects the healing love of Christ. To build such weapons of mass murder and to intend to use them is a sin against God and the human family.

The nuclear intention rooted in our hearts and the international arms race it has spawned claim hosts of victims each day. These are the victims of gross neglect, the starving of the world, many of whom are children, the little ones whom Jesus would welcome and touch (10:13). These victims are the marginal, the Galilean poor whose company he sought. They, the unfed, the diseased, the poor, become the holy innocents, living sacrifices before the nuclear idol.

How can we reconcile the victimhood of the starving and the suffering with our taking a place at table with Jesus? What does it mean to accept this eucharistic food while millions of sisters and brothers starve?

The eucharistic love that Jesus shares with us implies a risk. The mandate of eucharistic love is to be united with Christ and with one another. Despite the modern circumstances of betrayal and denial we face, we hear Jesus calling us to be servants of one another, members of his one body. When one person suffers we all suffer. As Christ had compassion for the hungry multitudes (6:30–44 and 8:1–10), we too are called to help feed one another. In fact, we are called to become Eucharist for one another in the midst of betrayal and denial. To be blessed, broken, and given for one another is to risk love at all costs.

Jesus died as he lived. With his arms outstretched on the Cross, totally disarmed, he embraces all humanity with his infinite, merciful love. Christ invites all of God's people to choose the path of love and self-sacrifice, which is the way of nonviolence, the true means of justice and peace. By identifying with the Suffering Servant, reconciliation and healing can occur between warring nations. Our allegiance to Jesus requires that we renounce our nuclear intention and remove the scandal of starvation from our world.

Faced with the violence of human starvation and nuclear annihilation we blindly insist "Surely not I, Lord!" At this moment Jesus offers us—as he did his disciples—communion in his mission of servanthood. United with Christ's sacrificial love, the hope of redemption and deliverance dawns anew for our world. We need only to risk incarnating the love of the Eucharist and place our complete trust in God. For Jesus assures us that "with God all things are possible" (10:27).

Discussion Questions

1.   (a) The Eucharist signifies our human brokenness and Christ's life broken for us on the Cross. Discuss the particular ways in which this brokenness is manifest in the world, in our lives, in the lives of those we know, in all the things that keep people separated and in fear. How do we all share in the disciples' betrayal of Christ?

(b) The Eucharist also signifies the spiritual food that nourishes us and brings us to wholeness and health. What vision for the world does the Eucharist present to the believer? Who belongs at the table? Who is to be fed? Who is to provide? The promises of the kingdom are beyond our wildest imaginings, so imagine boldly: What hopes for the world and for yourselves do you bring in coming to the Eucharist? Is there a risk in receiving the Eucharist if our aims are not consonant with Christ's?

2. Receiving the Eucharist unites us in Christ's universal, forgiving love. How then can we reconcile the presence of Christ's love in the Eucharist with our society's nuclear intention? Are there ways in which we can extend this eucharistic love as a healing force in a world of conflict and division?

3. While billions of dollars are spent each year on nuclear weapons, thousands of people suffer and die daily from neglect and lack of basic necessities. Discuss the connection between the nuclear arms race and the problem of world hunger and human need. Do you think our concern for security—both personally and as a nation—would become less and less important as we are willing to provide more and more for the just need of the world's poor? In what ways can the Eucharist enable us to share what we have with those who have little or nothing?

4. What is your reaction to Helen Caldicott's description of the growing prospects of nuclear war? Do you feel hopeful that nuclear war can be averted? Does your Christian faith contribute to the sense of hope that you might have? What changes do you think you can make in your life to work toward eliminating the threat of nuclear war?

Closing Reflection: Mark 14:22–25

During the meal he took bread, blessed and broke it, and gave it to them. "Take this," he said, "this is my body." He likewise took a cup, gave thanks and passed it to them, and they all drank from it. He said to them: "This is my blood, the blood of the covenant, to be poured out on behalf of many. I solemnly assure you, I will never again drink of the fruit of the vine until the day when I drink it new in the reign of God."

SESSION 5

A Liturgy of Life

Call to Worship

Let us seek to renew our commitment to follow Jesus, our crucified and risen Lord, by lifting up our lives in prayerful worship before God.

Opening Prayer

Nearing the end of our journey together, we echo the prayer of the blind Bartimaeus: "Jesus, Son of David, have mercy on (us)!" Our hearts are both burdened and blessed. The weight of our starving brothers and sisters, the enormity of our nuclear intention, and the ponderous danger of our nuclear arsenals bring us to our knees in prayer. Yet we have hope; we have your presence in the midst of our betrayal and denial; we have the promise of your empty tomb. You are going ahead of us, walking in the lead! Help us to follow in your footsteps. Cure our residual blindness so that we too can get up and follow you in the way of servanthood and reconciling love. Help us to recognize the areas of resistance in our hearts that still need your healing touch and those aspects of our thinking and acting that have yet to conform to your divine standards. As we reflect now on the path our discipleship should take in this nuclear age, we beg you, turn your loving attention to us as you did to Bartimaeus, and ask us as you did him: What would you have me do for you? Having walked with you these weeks, we do not ask for love without risks, but simply: Lord, that we might see! Amen.

Litany of Repentance and Hope

Jesus calls: "Reform your lives and believe in the gospel!" Faith in Christ requires converting our hearts and our hopes. It means giving testimony of our discipleship in a believing way of seeing, a hopeful way of judging, and a loving way of serving all of God's people in

38

Christ's name. Let us ask the Lord to pardon our failures of trust and fidelity and to set us on the path to life.

Response: LORD, LEAD US TO REPENTANCE

For questioning the authority of Jesus' teachings on the Cross, we ask you . . .

For placing human standards above divine compassion, we pray . . .

For the moral blindness of our nuclear intention, we beg you . . .

For trusting in instruments of death to save us rather than in the power of the Living God, we beseech you . . .

For betraying Christ's love in the Eucharist by allowing starvation to claim lives daily, we implore you . . .

For not fully believing that the Risen Christ is alive in our hearts, we plead . . .

Response: LORD, GIVE US HOPE

That we may become "new wineskins," fitting vessels of God's Spirit, we pray . . .

That our world—freed from armaments—may be a safe place to welcome children, we implore . . .

That touched by Christ, we may impart to others a vision of healing, we beg you . . .

That fear and selfishness may be converted through earnest and trusting prayer, we ask . . .

That we might risk extending to others the love and forgiveness Christ gives us in the Eucharist, we plead . . .

That embracing Christ's nonviolent way may lead us to new life, we beseech you . . .

Gospel Reading: Mark 16:1–8

16 THE WOMEN AT THE TOMB. [1] When the sabbath was over, Mary Magdalene, Mary the mother of James, and Salome brought perfumed oils with which they intended to go and anoint Jesus. ² Very early, just after sunrise, on the first day of the week they came to the tomb. ³ They were saying to one another, "Who will roll back the stone for us from the entrance to the tomb?" ⁴ When they looked, they found that the stone had been rolled back (it was a huge one). ⁵ On entering the tomb they saw a young man sitting at the right, dressed in a white robe. ⁶ This frightened them thoroughly, but he reassured them: "You need not be amazed! You are looking for Jesus of Nazareth, the one who was crucified. He has been raised up; he is not here. See the place where they laid him. ⁷ Go now and tell his disciples and Peter, 'He is going ahead of you to Galilee, where you will see him just as he told you.' " ⁸ They made their way out and fled from the tomb bewildered and trembling; and because of their great fear, they said nothing to anyone.

Seeing Beyond the Empty Tomb

Carrying perfumed oils, the faithful women make their way to the tomb of Jesus to serve him in death as they did in life. Their grief at the death of a loved one—a death by shameful public execution—is heavy. As they approach the tomb they worry: "Who will roll back the stone for us from the entrance of the tomb?" (16:3).

Who, we ask, will roll back the stone today? Christ is continuously executed in the ultimate death intention, the willingness to use nuclear weapons. The earth itself is becoming Christ's tomb. Who will roll away the stone of vengeance and empty the death threat of its power? The nuclear intention in our hearts and its infernal manifestations in our world are, it seems, too great to lift. For most of us, there is greater assurance in the power of nuclear weapons and military might than in our vulnerable faith in the power of Jesus and his Kingdom. The planetary tomb is becoming more tightly sealed; the cumulative history of human sinfulness increasingly conceals the power that could truly liberate us all. Our fears and hardness of heart seal up the life of Christ within us. We count him among the dead.

When the women look, they discover that the stone has been rolled back. The obstacle was in their mind, in their pessimistic expectation. They look to see a looming impediment, but instead they find something wholly different, the evidence of God's reign at hand. A new expectation comes alive in them as they look upon the empty tomb.

Penetrating faith is needed because the revelation of the power of

God's Kingdom at work is deep and mysterious. The empty tomb is the symbol of the resurrection. How paradoxical that emptiness should speak of God! Emptiness awes us, frightens us; it begs for something more. We think of empty missile silos and shudder at the prospect of explosive death. We think of empty grain silos and know that these signify despair for countless millions. Yet empty places often hide within them a seed that will grow unencumbered to fullness. Jesus' self-emptying love in life and death blossoms in fruitfulness from the empty tomb. His risen life conquers the emptiness of death. It is the death threat of Calvary that is hollow, not the promise of new life in Christ.

The rock set in place to guard the dead is a telling symbol of our blind faithlessness. Our pathetic deterrents designed to wall up our scarcely buried fears are powerless to make us secure. Jesus wants to break open these fetters to free us for a life beyond repressive fear. He invites us to empty ourselves of our paralyzing fear of death, of our need to lord it over others to make our importance felt, and of our desperate fear of being last and least.

Like the women at the tomb, our journey of discipleship will be rewarded when we look "for Jesus of Nazareth, the one who was crucified . . ." (16:6). To have Christian hope requires that the human, vulnerable, forgiving way of Christ becomes our way as well. It is significant that the Risen Lord, on the morning of his ultimate vindication, is called by the most human of titles. He is Jesus of Nazareth. The hometown name confirms his status as one of us, as a marginal Galilean. Even in triumph Jesus identifies with the last and the least, and to these he returns as he promised (16:7). Furthermore, Jesus is "the one who was crucified." The Cross of Jesus is not forgotten. Easter glory does not erase the wounds of unconditional love. Christ would have us remember both his limitless love and our complicity in the woundedness of our brothers and sisters.

"He has been raised up; he is not here. See the place where they laid him" (16:6). The empty tomb invites us to test our fragile faith. In discovering the empty tomb, we, like the women disciples, become frightened and amazed. Yet as we gaze into the emptiness, we are challenged to believe that Jesus is not among the dead but among the living. To believe that the crucified Nazarene has been raised to life gives us resurrected hearts. Our fears and amazement slowly dissipate giving way to the profound realization that Jesus is alive. This new-found hope revives our deadened hearts and our faith is revitalized. We become empowered to journey with Jesus beyond the empty tomb.

Jesus' journey beyond the tomb takes him back to Galilee, the place where his ministry began. It is there, the place of the outcasts and the neglected, to which Jesus returns to continue his mission of servant-hood. Jesus journeys ahead of us to this remote place and invites us to join him there. He promises us that if we embark on this pilgrimage of faith, we will *see* him. This promise gives us new hope. In this nuclear age, we can endure the challenges before us and be sustained in times of trial. We can fearlessly risk proclaiming with our lives that the way of the Cross is the means to true peace and new life. For Jesus, the Lord of Life, has gone ahead of us into the Galilees of our world and will be with us through our most perilous moments. To remind us of his constant guidance and sustenance on our journey, he has given us his Eucharist, the living food that endures forever. The promise of new life awaits us beyond the Cross. The challenge is to accept his invitation to discipleship and to journey with him wherever he calls us.

A Psalm of Peacemaking (Recite together)

We live in a time of kairos
    when humanity stands on the border of a promised time,
    when God's people are summoned to obedience and faithfulness
        to preserve God's creation,
        to stand with the poor and oppressed everywhere, and
        to stand together as the people of the earth;
    when with confession and with humility we repent of
        our blindness to the division and war in our own hearts and in
            our own land,
        our obsession with money and our pursuit of power,
        our irrational belief in security through weaponry, and
        our worship of secular gods.
We are called
    to be obedient to Jesus Christ, the Prince of Peace,
        who loves the whole world and
        who invites us to be stewards of the earth and servants of his
            people,
        to be co-workers in the new Creation.
Let us be peacemakers.

Let us be called the children of God,
    speaking boldly with moral conviction to the nation and to the
      world,
    building, with God's grace, a new moral order in the world com-
      munity; and
    acting now for world peace, an enterprise of justice, an outcome of
      love.

From "Peacemaking: The Believers' Calling," The United Presbyterian
Church in the United States of America, 1980

Offering of Intentions

Offering our prayers of commitment to be faithful disciples of Christ
in the nuclear age.

Lord's Prayer

Our Father, who art in heaven, hallowed be thy name; thy kingdom
come; thy will be done on earth as it is in heaven. Give us this day
our daily bread; and forgive us our trespasses as we forgive those who
trespass against us; and lead us not into temptation, but deliver us
from evil. For the kingdom, the power, and the glory are yours, now
and for ever.

Let us express to one another a sign of Christ's peace.

Sharing of the Eucharist

The Prayer of St. Francis of Assisi

Lord, make me an instrument of thy peace
    Where there is hatred, let me sow love;
    Where there is injury, pardon;
    Where there is doubt, faith;
    Where there is despair, hope;
    Where there is darkness, light;
And where there is sadness, joy.

O Divine Master, grant that I may not so much
    seek to be consoled as to console;
    to be understood as to understand;

to be loved as to love;
for it is in giving that we receive,
   it is in pardoning that we are pardoned,
   and it is in dying that we are born
   to eternal life.

Concluding Song

APPENDIX 1

The Courage to Start

THE COURAGE TO START
Robert C. Aldridge

Conversion—from being "thing-related" to being "people-centered"—seldom occurs in one cataclysmic flash of enlightenment but rather through a chain reaction of career-shocking, security-threatening experiences: experiences in love of others rather than the abstract morality that has corrupted this country since the first slave was sold.

To those of us of the World War II era, this transformation may be more painful; we have become further embedded in the mire of competition and personal gain. But it's no easy job for the youth of our nation either—many of whom are bathed in relative affluence.

My own questioning started one night several years ago. My oldest daughter and I were discussing campus activities against Dow Chemical, a company producing napalm for use in Vietnam. Our conversation then swung to my work at Lockheed: designing the Poseidon missile with its cluster of individually targeted re-entry vehicles, each carrying a nuclear warhead.

Showing real concern, she explained, "I'm worried, Dad. Pretty soon the demonstrations will be against *your* work."

That moved me because I saw her real worry was tied to a possible split between us over basic values—a split that might put us on opposite sides of the picket line. Of course I defended my position (which I truly believed at that time) that building deterrent weapons was holding off a hot war until cold-war differences were negotiated. I posed the problem of stopping our production when the Russians have engaged us in an arms race. Her contention was that someone must have the courage to start.

"Someone must have the courage to start." I could not shake that thought, and it troubled me. A good friend of mine once remarked that when a person made him uncomfortable, he found it advantageous to listen. I was more than uncomfortable—I was trapped. To complete my engineering studies, I had worked full time while attending college for five years. Since getting a degree, my advancement had been good—I was at that time leader of a design group for an advanced re-entry system. All my career preparation had been in this field, and I had worked hard. How could Janet, my wife, and I, with ten children, start over? Where do you get that kind of courage?

In spite of the seemingly formidable obstacles, a new consciousness had dawned on me. I became more aware of things happening at work. I noticed that most people did not really exhibit convictions of pursuing humanitarian projects to prevent war. That myth tinged our environment but was neither accepted nor rejected. It just hung there, unchallenged. Patriotic philosophies of defending our country were subordinated to concern for winning contracts or working more overtime.

I observed very little joy within the guarded gates of Lockheed. Only the intellectual side surfaced, and that was strictly along the lines of "me and my project." That attitude, along with tough-line competition for more responsibility, was the general rule. Motivation of people to gather more and more work under their wing amazed me. I finally diagnosed this "empire building" as groping for security—a need to become indispensable. But I knew of very few who actually achieved permanency: a budget cut or administrative reorganization could result in being declared "surplus" or squeezed out of line in the pecking order.

Potential insecurity and ruthless competition, coupled with the lack of personal satisfaction associated with pursuing wholesome tasks, are underlying reasons for the gloomy atmosphere. Constantly hanging over one's head is the negative force of fear. Lacking is the positive reward of seeing one's labor benefit humanity. I did not realize it at the time but my interior self was changing from the "I-It" to the "I-Thou" attitude—the death knell of an engineering career in the defense industry.

Had I been more alert, I would have recognized harbingers of this human concern shining through my mechanized mentality sooner. A conversation many years ago, shortly after I started work at Lockheed, still lurks in my memory—probably because I realized in my subconscious that it was never completed.

I had engaged one of my colleagues in a philosophical discussion of religion and its meaning in daily life. He asked: "What do you think God wants you to do most of all?" "Just what I am doing," I responded spontaneously, "to help build this missile to protect our country."

He commented that I was fortunate in my conviction and the conversation died. But that dialogue continued to make me think. Was he beginning to struggle within himself? Or was it just a casual question with an offhand response? Whatever, it disturbed me. But I had not yet learned to listen when disturbed.

Gradually my awareness of surroundings developed into curiosity as patterns unfolded before me. I saw behind-the-scenes activity associated with the daily newscast. I witnessed a task force set up to circumvent what good might come from negotiations to stop the arms race. I saw numerous violations of the test ban treaty when underground nuclear explosions vented into the Nevada atmosphere. Reports I read indicated we could safely negotiate an antiballistic-missile freeze because, in addition to being ineffective, our Safeguard system was too expensive and too controversial to be deployed. Finally, when I saw the trend toward greater accuracy and greater warhead yield—a potential shift from the retaliatory deterrent to a first-strike weapon—I became really uneasy. All this undermining of sincerity at the negotiating table was being kept secret from the American people and the reasons were obvious: bureaucracy and profits. With access to inside knowledge it was not difficult for me to deduce that we had already reached the saturation point of deterrent capability.

A temporary outlet was involvement in the peace movement. As peace information coordinator for the National Association of Laity (NAL), I was exposed to more study and research and this time it reached international dimensions. I avidly pursued investigation on how American institutions affect underdeveloped countries. New knowledge of how the corporate pattern (in which I had become so deeply enmeshed) was repressing poor people at home and abroad made my complicity more untenable.

So I built bombs as a profession and worked for peace as a hobby—an existence I pursued openly by taking part in all public peace activities. There was a dormant desire that the FBI would find me out and cancel my security clearance. That would make the decision for me, but they never tumbled. During the NAL convention on peace at New York's Fordham University, I was introduced to the assembly as a Lockheed defense worker. Several men approached me afterward to ask questions regarding my conflict of interest, but apparently they weren't Hoover's men as nothing further came of it. My decision of conscience would not be made by default.

Eventually my peace-seeking activities turned in on me. One can only go so far in quest of justice without coming to terms with his own living pattern. In early 1972 Janet and I started planning for the transition. We itemized objectives, areas to investigate, library research, and people with whom we should discuss our plans. These were all outlined as short-term goals—we would schedule ongoing activity after the investigation phase. Our plan proceeded well until events accelerated our decision.

In August of that same year, Janet and I were sent to Honolulu to offer NAL support during the "Hickam Three" trial. The defendants were members of the Catholic Action of Hawaii, an NAL chapter. Attempting to spark consciousness in the people, the accused poured their own blood over top-secret electronic warfare files at Hickam Air Base, intelligence and targeting center for the Indochina air war. Their words during the pouring illustrate their intense motivation:

> *We pour our blood in the name of the God of Love, who lives now in the world in the maimed flesh of suffering people. . .*
> *We pour our blood to signify the responsibility of American citizens for the most terrible atrocities since Nazi Germany's gas chambers. . .*
> *We pour our blood, finally, in the name of the human family under God, a global community created to live in peace, in brotherhood and sisterhood—a community of love which can become fully real only when we are willing to resist the shedding of others' blood by the giving of our own.*

First hand contact with people who jeopardized their liberty for the suffering in the world caused me to quickly single out the double standard in my own life. It was then that I realized the date for ending my complicity in a program of destruction must be set and that date must be soon. Prolonging this decision was compromising my human integrity. "Someone must have the courage to start."

The Honolulu experience filled another need I felt necessary at that time. Up until then, all those I knew who had uprooted their life resisting immorality did not have families. With six children still living at home I could not completely relate to their actions. Now I had met a person who furnished a precedent. James W. Douglass—theologian, advisor to bishops during Vatican II, author, university professor, and "Hickam Three" defendant—is a husband and father of a family. Later, while reading Jim's book *Resistance and Contemplation: the Way of Liberation,* I could see where he had also struggled with a concern for his family and solved it:

> *I fear what they can do to me. It is a fear which runs from my seeing it directly, but a fear which I feel identifying itself with all that I have now and would lose—if my fear should be realized, and they should take it all away.*
> Take what away?
> *Everything I have.*
> Like what, for example?
> *Well, if you want an inventory: job, home, friends, reputation, a way of life which adds up to a secure existence for my family and myself. I fear much more for my wife and family than I do for myself. I have no right to neglect their needs because of my own feelings of conscience. My first duty is to my wife and family.*
> Your wife is as capable as you are of resistance. Women and men resist together in Indochina. It is in America that men feel such unique obligations toward women: pots and pans for the American woman, napalm for the Vietnamese. Let your family—wife, husband and children together—be a family of resistance. Grant them all the dignity of entering the real world, where most families suffer while yours prospers.

Jim's dialogue with Jesus made me ashamed. I had voiced those same fears and asked those same questions but I hadn't listened well enough to the answers. I had to see someone actually try the road before I could venture on it. We Christians lean too much on precedents which are merely crutches to bolster our weak determination. We must learn to have confidence in our own convictions. Our subjective morality must yield to a contemporary pattern of spiritual activity.

We set the date for January of 1973. Immediately after Christmas vacation I would give notice of my resignation. We would start the new year with a new life.

The four days following Christmas were set aside as a period of family contemplation to unify and crystalize our intentions as a family of resistance. We rented a mountain cabin and retired in wilderness seclusion to read and talk. We were trying to center moral teachings and biblical lessons on our family and how we should face the future. We were building spiritual strength to weather the trying times ahead.

On January 2, 1973, I tendered my resignation. We were now past the point of no return. During that last month I discussed my action with my co-workers. Some agreed with me and would like to do the same but the needs for security are too strong. That singular fear is the main obstacle to moral action. Theologians have developed theologies of liberation and theologies of civil disobedience, but we still need a theology of courage. It must tangibly relate to the working person with a family and be something more than general rules and abstract teaching; it must be brought alive in shops and offices.

So now I am liberated from the military-industrial complex. Our family is still going through the pain of adjustment. After 25 years of homemaking, Janet now works part time helping children. I am motivated to do freelance writing because I feel there are things I must say. The kids have taken on more responsibility at home and are growing in self-reliance.

The way ahead is still foggy but, as I told my colleague many years ago, I am doing what I think God wants me to do. We are relying on faith—a faith in ourselves and what we believe and a faith that a force is moving us as long as we, in our free will, respond. Life is scary now. I'm beginning to understand what Daniel Berrigan called "the dark night of resistance" and what Thomas Merton meant when he wrote, "Divine light of faith is thick darkness to the soul."

Well, someone must have the courage.

Reprinted from *Fellowship,* April 1976. Available from Fellowship Publications, Box 271, Nyack, N.Y. 10960.

Robert Aldridge worked 16 years as an aerospace engineer for Lockheed Missiles and Space Company. When he resigned because of conscientious objection to war, he was group leader responsible for design on the MK 500 MaRV (Maneuvering Re-entry Vehicle), a type of missile with multiple warheads that can be used with extreme accuracy and which has a first-strike military potential. He is now a member of the Pacific Life Community and the Fellowship of Reconciliation. An outspoken critic against "first-strike" nuclear weapons, Aldridge has published *The Counterforce Syndrome* and *First Strike.*

APPENDIX 2

The Nuclear Arms Race

History of the Nuclear Arms Race · 52

Action-Reaction Cycle in the Nuclear Competition · 58

The New Generation of Nuclear Weapons · 59

Nuclear War by Computer Chip · 64

Glossary of Key Nuclear Arms Race Terminology · 68

HISTORY OF THE NUCLEAR ARMS RACE
Richard J. Barnet

The First Arms Race

The United States first developed nuclear weapons in 1945 for the purpose of winning the war against Japan. We did not have any theory of deterrence. In fact, we had very little theory about it at all. The atomic bomb, as President Truman said, was just another piece of artillery, and to his dying day he contended that nothing much had changed: weapons had only gotten bigger, not different.

As the arms race began to develop, the United States was always first with the latest technology. We were the first to develop the atomic bomb, the long-range bomber, a deliverable hydrogen bomb—although the Soviets exploded theirs first, a new hydra-headed multiple-warhead missile (MIRV), the Cruise missile, and so forth. At every stage during this first arms race, the Soviet Union, usually some five years later, duplicated the technological achievements on which the United States had hoped to base its security.

I would agree with Jerome Wiesner, who was President Kennedy's science advisor and is now president of MIT, that this arms race, lasting from 1945 to 1962, was a race that we were running with ourselves. We know now beyond doubt that the Soviet Union was not in the same race. It had neither the capability, nor the funds, nor the national organization after suffering the catastrophic damage of World War II in which twenty million Soviet citizens were killed, to match the United States bomb for bomb or dollar for ruble. The situation was rather asymmetrical. The United States was building a military force which every President said had to be "second to none," and the Soviet Union was developing the same technology very slowly, not attempting to match the United States but rather trying to substitute public relations and bluff for the expenditure of money and the amassing of a huge arsenal.

This was the era of Nikita Khrushchev, who every few years would come out with a pungent statement about Soviet weapons. Their missiles, he said, would hit a fly in outer space. He was producing missiles like sausages—although it turned out that in those days they weren't producing any sausages—but we didn't get the point. However, we got the point they wanted us to get, thanks in large part to the best public relations firm that money could buy—the Department of Defense—whose interest was the same as Khrushchev's, namely, to let everybody think that the Soviets had a big army and a big missile system because that would scare away an attack. The Defense Department also wanted to paint an exaggerated picture of Soviet strength to justify bigger military budgets—and they still do! Neither the Soviet Union nor the United States was really planning to attack the other.

There was deterrence on both sides, but they were deterring different things. The United States, with its huge nuclear arsenal—which today has reached a level of thirty thousand weapons—was trying to deter Soviet political operations. We wanted to make them cautious about exploiting the vulnerable political situation in Western Europe, which many people in the United States government feared would bring Communist governments to power, because in 1947 there were already Communists in the cabinets of Italy and France. So initially, the whole nuclear weapons theory involved developing a power that would keep the Soviet Union from challenging the United States in areas of the world where we did not want that to happen—which was virtually everywhere.

The Soviet Union, on the other hand, was trying to deter an attack on the Soviet Union. From their point of view, the situation in 1948 was extremely dangerous. The United States had a monopoly of nuclear weapons; there was a cold war and a high level of public fear, even hysteria, in the United States. There were many signs of that fear and a total obsession with the Soviet Union. There was an entire issue of *Collier's* weekly magazine in 1949 devoted to the coming war and defeat of the Soviet Union. It described in detail how the United States would bomb the Soviet Union, occupy it, and then reeducate the people in the religion of free enterprise. And if that was not scary enough, we had a Secretary of the Navy and some generals who made statements during this same period about the necessity, inevitability, and even legitimacy of fighting a so-called "preventative" war. Since the Soviet Union was always paranoid about its security, after wave upon wave of foreign invasions over the centuries, the leaders were frightened and determined to produce the bomb themselves. Every scientist who worked on the atomic bomb testified year after year that an arms race with the Soviet Union was inevitable. There was no doubt that they were going to match us in weapons development.

In the first arms race, the United States had to prove that our nuclear arsenal was credible. It was not only important that we had the weapons, but we also had to demonstrate the will to use them. Many people in this country labor under the illusion that these weapons are not meant to be used. The fact is that people go to work every day, operating on precisely the opposite assumption. And indeed there have been several incidents, particularly in this first arms race, when the possible use of nuclear weapons was considered at an extremely high level of command.

Nuclear War as Strategy

In 1954, according to French Foreign Minister George Bidault, Secretary of State John Foster Dulles offered to drop one or more atomic bombs on Communist Chinese territory near the Indo-China border and two atomic bombs against the Vietminh at Dien Bien Phu. Such a historical reminder ought to make us realize how absurd this nuclear arms race is. The Chinese Communists, whom we were seriously considering destroying with a nuclear strike, are now close to becoming allies of the United States.

Here is another example: President Eisenhower, looking back to his arrival at the White House in 1953, said, "I let it be known that if there was not going to be an armistice (this was in Korea) . . . we were not going to be bound by the kind of weapons that we would use. . . . I don't mean to say that we'd have used those big things and destroyed cities," Eisenhower added, "but we would have used enough to win, and we of course would have tried to keep them on military, not civil targets."*

Here is a third example: In October 1962, at the time of the Cuban missile crisis, the United States initiated a blockade of Cuba and prepared for an invasion, knowing that there were substantial risks of nuclear war. "We all agreed in the end," Robert Kennedy said afterward, "that if the Russians were willing to go to nuclear war over Cuba, it meant that they were ready to go to nuclear war, and that was that; so they might as well have the showdown then, instead of six months later." And that, I suggest, is exactly how a nuclear war can come about. In my view, the only time a leader will deliberately initiate a nuclear war is when the situation, in his mind, is "nuclear war now or later—better now."

One member of the Joint Chiefs of Staff, Kennedy recalled, felt that we could use nuclear weapons because our adversaries would use theirs against us in an attack. And in 1961 the Kennedy Administration seriously contemplated the use of nuclear weapons during the Berlin crisis in which U.S. and Soviet tanks faced each other in the center of the city.

Even earlier, Douglas MacArthur had proposed using nuclear weapons in Korea. And in 1968, as General William Westmoreland writes in his memoirs, he convened a small secret group in Saigon to study the nuclear defense of Khe Sanh, where the Marine base was in imminent danger of being overrun. Even now, he still thinks that using a few small, tactical nuclear weapons in Vietnam—or even threatening to use them—might have brought the war to an earlier end.

The Second Arms Race

The first arms race ended with the Cuban missile crisis. The Russians found that the policy of bluff did not work, so Khrushchev the money-saver was thrown out, and there began the armament build-up which continues to this day. The Soviet Union has been steadily building in areas of intercontinental missiles and in the development of its forces in central Europe. It has matched or, perhaps in a purely military sense, even exceeded the United States in certain areas. But the major point is that the military build-up on both sides has been so great that the difference between the thirty thousand nuclear weapons that the United States has and the roughly twenty thousand that the Soviet Union has is meaningless.

More important are the Soviet submarines off the coast of the United States, carrying about two hundred nuclear weapons, each targeted on an American city and each capable of destroying an American city. The fact that the United States has submarines off the coast of the Soviet Union with three thousand nuclear weapons does not make us one bit safer. The numbers already developed have reached the point where the numbers game is an activity for fools and spendthrifts, not for people who are really interested in saving society or in security for themselves and their families.

*Sidney Lens, *The Day Before Doomsday* (New York: Doubleday, 1977), p. 119.

The second arms race started with the Soviet buildup which launched the negotiations that we call SALT (Strategic Arms Limitation Talks). For many years, as we all know, there have been negotiations for the purpose of limiting future arms build-ups. But during the years of SALT, not one single weapon has been destroyed, and in fact, stockpiles on both sides have doubled and new weapons have been developed.

Today's Arms Race

Most importantly, these have been the years of the major technological developments which have caused the situation I mentioned at the outset and which make the world that we have come through look like a Quaker village in comparison. This third arms race is not just a race of numbers—we have had enough of those numbers to see that they hardly matter. The difference today is in the nature of the technology and of the military doctrine supporting and justifying that technology.

We have both sides—and again the United States is ahead in terms of time and energy—pushing toward highly accurate systems, which means an extremely dangerous situation. These highly accurate warheads, sensitive gear for fighting computer-programmed limited nuclear wars, new and more powerful intercontinental missiles, lasers, killer satellites, and other so-called "war-winning technology" make the military environment far less stable today than it has ever been.

Military planners on both sides are under increasing pressures to keep their forces at a high state of alertness, and simply to resolve the "doubts" that come up all the time—flocks of geese on the radar screen, computer mistakes and breakdowns. All the things that happen in department-store billing departments can happen, of course, in military systems too. With all these human and mechanical errors that are possible, the temptation would be in favor of launching the missiles. We are living in a world where missiles are being programmed to hit missiles; so the premium on going first is enormous. These pressures are making the world a much more dangerous place than it has been at any time since the dawn of the nuclear era.

War by Miscalculation

In the final analysis, the fight between the doves and the hawks has very little to do with technology or numbers of weapons. It is important to know about weapons systems, and not very hard, although the subject is one of the most mythicized in the world. Almost any other issue of modern-day living— whether it is figuring out how to get water to our cities, energy, housing, transportation—has far more intellectual content. And these involve much more difficult problems than the subject of the arms race, as far as talking about what to do. But that is not the issue. What really is at stake here is a fundamental disagreement about human nature.

Our whole nuclear weapons system is based on a view of the Russian leaders sitting by a computer, calculating each day how many weapons we have, how many weapons they have, what the winds will look like on the day of the nuclear war, what the effects will be on the water and transportation systems, how many people will die from radiation. Then some day, the computer will show a magic number of "acceptable casualties"—it may be ten million, twenty million, or fifty million, depending on how evil and sick we think they are. But on that day, they will decide that running a world with the United States out of the way is worth launching a nuclear war. Unless you believe that fantasy of how human beings behave in general, and how these particular Russian leaders are likely to behave in particular, the whole theory behind the amassing of nuclear weapons, the whole justification for building a single additional weapon—or for not destroying half or more of what we have—fades away.

It is not a plausible scenario for nuclear war, but by believing the fantasy and by acting it, we make other scenarios far more plausible. War by miscalculation—this happens when one side or the other says, "It's now or never; we are on an inevitable collision course." The issue becomes, not war or peace, but war now or war then. That is when one side or the other makes the major miscalculation. Every war is a war of miscalculation. In the First World War, if you have read Barbara Tuchman's account, one side made a move expecting the other side to back down, and the other side did not. The Russians have done a lot of backing down in major confrontations, but there is no reason to believe that they will always do so in the future.

At the dawn of the nuclear age, Albert Einstein, who not only developed the theory that made the bomb possible, but also wrote the letter launching its production in the United States, said, "Everything is changed except our way of thinking." We have the same habits of mind today in thinking about security and defense that we have had all through history, from the days of bows and arrows to tanks and armies. But times have changed, and if we are going to survive, we must learn that our real strength is not in these useless and dangerous missiles that sooner or later will surely kill us.

Our strength lies in the people who can create, not destroy, who can be proud and free, and who are working to find a way to make a world that they really can leave to their children. This generation has, quite humbly, the final responsibility and the last chance to turn terror into hope.

From *Peace in Search of Makers,* Jane Rockman, editor (Valley Forge, Pa.: Judson Press, 1979). Used by permission of Judson Press.

Richard J. Barnet is co-founder of the Institute for Political Studies, Washington, D.C., a former Kennedy White House staff member, and author of *Global Reach* and *Roots of War.*

Nuclear Weapons Tests
1945–1978

Nuclear weapons testing has played a critical role in the continued research and development of nuclear weapons and their delivery systems by the handful of nuclear nations. Between the years 1945 and 1978 there were 1,165 nuclear explosions produced by five nuclear weapons states, 89% of them by the superpowers. Rising concern about the radioactive fallout associated with the tests led in 1963 to a treaty prohibiting tests in the atmosphere, outer space, or under water. The treaty was successful in halting atmospheric testing by the signatory nations, but did not slow the pace of experimentation. A comprehensive ban that would prohibit underground testing as well is still under negotiation.

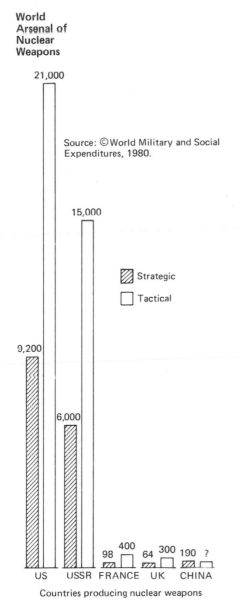

World Arsenal of Nuclear Weapons

Source: © World Military and Social Expenditures, 1980.

Countries producing nuclear weapons

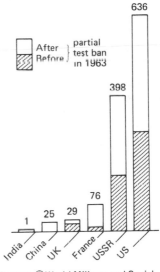

Source: © World Military and Social Expenditures, 1979.

ACTION-REACTION CYCLE
IN THE NUCLEAR COMPETITION

The dynamics of the nuclear arms race ensure that development of a new weapons system by one power will in a relatively brief period be followed by a comparable achievement by the other. Both powers have had "firsts." Neither has stayed ahead for long. The US generally has a technological lead of several years, but the futility of the race for short-term advantage is demonstrated by a chronology of developments to date.

US 1945   **atomic bomb**   *1949 USSR*

The nuclear age began with the explosion of a US A-bomb of 12.5 kilotons (equivalent to 12,500 tons of TNT) over Hiroshima, Japan. The single bomb, which destroyed the city, introduced to the world a concentrated explosive force of unprecedented power. Within four years, the USSR conducted its first atomic test.

US 1948   **intercontinental bomber**   *1955 USSR*

By 1948, the US had begun to replace the propeller planes of World War II with long-range jets. The first planes developed for strategic (intercontinental) bombing required refueling to reach another continent. In 1955, the US began deployment of the all-jet intercontinental bomber, and USSR soon followed suit.

US 1954   **hydrogen bomb**   *1955 USSR*

The H-bomb multiplied the explosive force of the A-bomb 1,000 times. The first US thermonuclear bomb had a yield equivalent to 15,000,000 tons of TNT; a year later the USSR tested a bomb in the million-ton range.

intercontinental ballistic missile
USSR 1957   **(ICBM)**   *1958 US*

Following intensive development by both nuclear powers, a land-based missile to carry nuclear warheads intercontinental distances was successfully flight-tested by the USSR in 1957, and by the US a year later. By 1962 both nations had ICBM's with a range of 6,000 miles, each missile able to carry a payload equivalent to 5-10,000,000 tons of TNT.

USSR 1957   **human-made satellite in orbit**   *1958 US*

Sputnik I by the USSR initiated a space race which quickly took on military functions; the first US satellite was launched into orbit the following year. Through 1979 more than half the superpowers' satellites have been military: for surveillance, targeting, etc.

submarine-launched ballistic
US 1960   **missile (SLBM)**   *1968 USSR*

A nuclear-powered submarine which could fire long-range missiles from a submerged position was the third means of strategic delivery. The US produced the nuclear-powered Polaris, with missiles with a range of 1,200 nautical miles. Eight years later the USSR had comparable nuclear subs.

US 1966   multiple warhead (MRV)   1968 USSR
Multiheaded missiles increased the number of targets a missile could hit. US MRV'd missiles carried three warheads, each with sixteen times the explosive force of the Hiroshima bomb. The USSR had them two years later.

USSR 1968   anti-ballistic missile (ABM)   1972 US
The USSR deployed 64 defensive missiles around Moscow. The US began construction of the Safeguard system in 1969 and had one site completed when a treaty restricting ABM's was signed in 1972. Generally judged militarily ineffective, ABM's were restricted to one site in each country in 1974. Subsequently the US site was closed.

multiple independently-targeted
US 1970   warhead (MIRV)   1975 USSR
Further development of multiple warheads enabled one missile to hit three to ten individually selected targets as far apart as 100 miles. USSR began to flight-test MIRV's three years after US put them in service; in 1976, USSR deployed the six-headed SS-19.

US 198?   new long-range cruise missile   198? USSR
Adaptable to launching from air, sea, and land, a new generation of long-range missiles is under development. The cruise missile is small, relatively inexpensive, highly accurate, with the unique advantage of very low trajectory. Following the contours of the earth, and flying under radar, it will be able to destroy its target without warning. The US is in the lead in this technology.

Source: World Military Expenditures, 1979, by Ruth Leger Sivard ⓒ 1979 World Priorities, Box 1003, Leesburg, Va. 22075

THE NEW GENERATION OF NUCLEAR WEAPONS

The escalating nuclear arms race between the U.S. and the USSR threatens to bring the human venture to an end. The two superpowers are now locked into a hostile "action-reaction" cycle that could easily produce a military collision eventually ending in nuclear confrontation. With the development of a new generation of nuclear weapons by the U.S. and the USSR, both sides are rapidly gaining "first-strike" capability—the ability to destroy military targets (i.e., missile sites, military bases)—with precise accuracy. While the U.S. leads the Soviets in acquiring a "first-strike" nuclear triad of air-, land-, and sea-based missiles, the Soviets are quickly developing a "first-strike" capability to counteract the U.S. This "first-strike" capability tends to reinforce the concept of "limited nuclear war," a concept increasingly accepted by military planners. Currently the USSR and the U.S. add three to ten nuclear weapons to their stockpiles each day. The U.S. possesses some 30,000 nuclear warheads, capable of destroying every major Soviet city 40 times over. The USSR has approximately 21,000 nuclear warheads, capable of destroying every major U.S. city 26 times over.

Nonnuclear or conventional military confrontations that could evolve between the superpowers or other nuclear nations also enhance the likelihood of a potential nuclear exchange. The revival of cold war sentiment between the superpowers and their allies has been caused by the following developments: failure of the SALT process to create a climate of trust and to substantially reduce nuclear weapons research, testing, and development; concern in Western Europe over the Soviet build-up of SS-20 missiles; intense U.S. pressure on the NATO countries to increase their military spending and deploy a new line of strategic nuclear weapons; U.S. rejection of the Soviet offer to negotiate mutual reductions; the beginnings of a new Sino-American alignment; and an increased military presence by the Soviet Union and the United States in Southwest Asia and the oil-rich region of the Persian Gulf.

This overview outlines the major U.S., USSR, and European nuclear weapons developments and capabilities in the 1980s.

U.S. Nuclear Weapons Developments

The current government plan for the military calls for the authority to spend over $1 trillion from 1981 through 1985. This new surge in military spending includes massive funding for *counterforce* or "first-strike" nuclear weapons systems. These first-strike weapons are described below.

Trident Submarine—A nuclear-powered submarine over two football fields long and five stories high. A single Trident missile, if launched, can travel over half of the world's surface within a quarter of an hour and strike within a few feet of its target. Presently, three Tridents are at various stages of production, and two are nearly ready for active duty. Until the Trident II missile is developed sometime between 1982–1983, the Trident I missile is slated for use in the Trident and some Poseidon nuclear war submarines, Trident's predecessor. The Trident I missile will have between 10–12 warheads per missile, while the Trident II missile will contain 14–17 warheads. A single Trident submarine equipped with Trident II missiles will be able to destroy 408 cities of 100,000 people each or any structurally reinforced military targets with a blast five times greater than the bomb dropped on Hiroshima.

Projected cost: Over $1.7 billion apiece. More than $8 billion has already been spent. The Navy wants a fleet of over 20 Tridents. The entire project if completed could cost over $30 billion.

Primary Contractors: General Dynamics, Electric Boat Division, Groton, Conn. and San Diego, Calif.; IBM Corp., Manassas, Va.; Lockheed Aircraft Corp., Sunnyvale, Calif.; RCA Corp., Camden, N.J.; Rockwell

Intl., Anaheim, Calif.; Singer Co., Glendale, Calif. and Wayne, N.J.; Sperry Rand Corp., Great Neck, N.Y.; Westinghouse Electric Corp., Sunnyvale, Calif.; United Technologies Corp., Sunnyvale, Calif.

M-X Missile—A land-based intercontinental ballistic missile (ICBM) carrying 10 to 14 independently targeted warheads. These missiles are extremely accurate, being able to travel 7,000 miles and come literally within several yards of their target. These missiles are projected to be placed on moving vehicles and stored in easily accessible silos in the states of Utah and Nevada.

Projected Cost: $100 million per missile, between $30–50 billion for the entire project. Over $160 million has already been spent.

Primary Contractors: Aerojet General Corp., Sacramento, Calif.; Northrop Corp., Hawthorne, Calif.; Ralph M. Parsons, Los Angeles, Calif.; Boeing Co., Seattle, Wash.

Cruise Missile—A small, subsonic, pilotless jet airplane, 14 to 20 feet long, which is programmed to fly a prescribed route and then to destroy its intended target. It flies at tree-top level, eluding enemy radar, and is guided to its target by computer. The Cruise missile can be launched from almost any military vehicle on land, in the air, or in the sea. Air-launch cruise missiles will be retrofitted to existing bomber aircraft, such as the B-52.

Projected Cost: More than $8 billion for the entire project.

Primary Contractors: Boeing Co., Seattle, Wash.; General Dynamics, San Diego, Calif.; McDonnell Douglas Corp., St. Louis, Mo.; Williams Research, Walled Lake, Mich.

Neutron Bomb—An "enhanced radiation" weapon, the neutron bomb is a small "low-yield" nuclear bomb. Its special shielding mechanisms reduce the blast effect but increase the release of radiation energy in the form of neutrons. Thus, this weapon kills by neutron radiation while minimizing property destruction.

Projected Cost: Over $1 billion has been allocated to research the neutron bomb.

Primary Contractors: Because this project is in the research stage, the specific contractors are not readily accessible from the Department of Defense or the Department of Energy.

Mark 12-A Reentry Vehicle—The basic MIRV warhead developed and deployed by the U.S. The Mark 12-A carries a hydrogen bomb equivalent to 335 kilotons. Three of these warheads are being placed on each of the Minuteman III ICBM's. With its new NS-20 guidance system, the Mark 12-A will have a precision accuracy and an enormous explosive power capable of destroying missile silos and other military targets. The Mark

12-A warhead is also projected to be used as part of the Trident II missile as well as the M-X missile, both being first-strike weapons.

Projected Cost: According to the U.S. General Accounting Office, over $500 million has been earmarked for the development of the Mark 12-A through 1982. More than $87 million has been allocated for 1981.

Primary Contractor: General Electric, Bangor, Wa., Pittsfield, Ma., Philadelphia, Pa., King of Prussia, Pa.

Soviet Nuclear Weapons Developments

According to the Stockholm International Peace Research Institute (SIPRI) the USSR has in operation and under continued production a series of multiple-warhead ICBMs capable of destroying a high percentage of U.S. fixed ICBMs. The new Soviet-based ICBMs—the SS-17, SS-18 and SS-19 land-based missiles—are ostensibly a response to the U.S. deployment in the early 1970s of multiple-warhead ICBMs—the Minutemen III force. These new Soviet ICBMs have a 7,000-mile range and carry 8 nuclear warheads. Compared to the accuracy Soviet ICBM warheads will have, the new U.S. Mark 12-A warhead will have an 80 percent chance of destroying any military targets, according to Pentagon calculations. A report that appeared in the May 9, 1977, issue of *Time* magazine submitted that the SS-18 has a 60 percent chance of destroying its target.

The sea-based leg of the Soviet nuclear triad as described in Robert C. Aldridge's book, *The Counterforce Syndrome,* consists of the Delta I and Delta II submarines. The first 13 Delta submarines had 12 launch tubes with each missile having a 4,200 mile range. In 1976 the Delta II emerged, which contains 16 missiles and has a range of about 4,800 miles. Compared to the Delta II, the U.S. Trident submarine has a greater destructive power and accuracy. To counteract the U.S. development of the Trident II missile, the Soviets are now developing the SS-NX-18, a missile similar to the Trident II but with fewer warheads and a lesser degree of accuracy.

Other new developments in the Soviet military arsenal as reported by SIPRI include the deployment of medium and intermediate range nuclear weapon delivery systems. The Soviet SS-20 missile, which can carry 3 independently targetable nuclear warheads to ranges up to 2,800 miles, substantially increases the Soviet Union's nuclear potential in Europe. Another Soviet Euro-strategic weapon that continues to be developed is the Tu22M Backfire bomber, which is capable of carrying out intercontinental missions. By and large, these Soviet nuclear weapon developments represent an increase in potential first-strike technology, a shift in policy and technology that mirrors a similar U.S. shift in the early and mid-1970s.

Projected Cost: Due to the unavailability of a reliable breakdown of the Soviet military budget, the costs of specific Soviet nuclear weapons systems are difficult to verify. SIPRI however estimates that Soviet military expenditures in 1979 were 23.7 percent of total world military expenditures or over $113 billion. Like the U.S. military budget, the Soviet military budget is expected to increase annually at a rate over the cost of inflation, with large outlays for the development of first-strike nuclear weapons.

Eurostrategic Nuclear Weapons Developments

Under intense U.S. pressure, North Atlantic Treaty Organization (NATO) countries agreed in December 1979 to deploy 108 new Pershing II nuclear ballistic missiles and 464 ground-launched nuclear Cruise missiles, enabling U.S. and NATO forces to launch a hair-trigger, first-strike attack against military bases and missile sites in the western part of the Soviet Union. NATO plans to station the new missiles in Belgium, West Germany, the United Kingdom, and possibly the Netherlands and Italy. United States and NATO planners claim that these new Eurostrategic weapons are needed to counter the Soviet Union's Backfire bomber and medium-range SS-20 missiles. However, the Soviets claim that these weapons were deployed to offset the imbalance, created by the U.S. forward-based system of air-deployment sites and fighter bombers, which ring the Soviet Union.

There is at present an approximate nuclear balance in Europe, consisting mostly of tactical nuclear weapons. However, if NATO deploys the new strategic weapons in 1983, as currently planned, any hope of negotiating arms reductions in Europe will be critically undercut. There is strong popular resistance to the new missiles in several European countries. Many Europeans criticize the NATO decision to ignore the Soviet unilateral withdrawal of troops from the German Democratic Republic in the fall of 1979, as well as the expressed willingness of the Soviets to negotiate further reductions.

Projected Cost: The cost of developing and deploying these missiles is over $5 billion.

Source for "U. S. Nuclear Weapons Developments" and for "Eurostrategic Nuclear Weapons Developments": National Action/Research on the Military-Industrial Complex (NARMIC), 1501 Cherry Street, Philadelphia, Pa. 19102.

THE NUCLEAR CLUB

Countries that have built and tested nuclear devices:	Those believed capable of building a nuclear bomb:	Potential developers of a nuclear bomb in five to ten years:
United States	Brazil	Pakistan
USSR	Argentina	Iraq
Britain	Israel	Libya
France	Canada	Egypt
China	South Africa	Japan
India	West Germany	Taiwan
	Sweden	South Korea

Source: Arms Control Association, Washington, D.C.

NUCLEAR WAR
BY COMPUTER CHIP:
HOW AMERICA ALMOST 'LAUNCHED ON WARNING'
Richard Thaxton

Fittingly enough, *Dr. Strangelove* was showing at the Capitol Hill Cinema in Washington June 6 [1980] when a false alarm of a massive Soviet attack—the second in a week and the third in seven months—started the countdown for an American nuclear strike against Russia.

In *Strangelove,* it took a mad SAC general, a Soviet doomsday device, and a bizarre series of accidents and miscalculations to ignite World War III.

The two most recent false alarms were set off by something far simpler—a short-circuit in a computer chip the size of a dime and worth less than half a dollar. In both alerts, the error was detected in three minutes, but not before U.S. nuclear armaments were unsheathed.

Could the Pentagon's errant, forty-six-cent computer chip actually have triggered doomsday with a premature warning that it had come? Defense Secretary Harold Brown answered this question with an emphatic "no." He said the warning system's safeguards require absolute verification of any attack and prevent machines from usurping the ultimate decision to retaliate.

Unfortunately, Brown's assessment seems much too sanguine in light of the escalating U.S.-Soviet rift, the march of nuclear weapons technology, and his own admission that false alarms of atomic attack are likely to recur.

Herbert Scoville is one of several defense experts who believe the two June false alarms were considerably more dangerous than the one that occurred last November 9. Tension had heightened over the months because of the Soviet invasion of Afghanistan and President Carter's warning that the United States would resort to force—possibly nuclear force—if the Russians were to move on the Persian Gulf.

Some officials say the intense preparations for war taken during the brief June false alarms suggest the United States is on a higher level of alert than in November—that the situation is now "hair trigger."

The November 9 alarm, also caused by a computer error, lasted twice as long as the two in June. Yet SAC nuclear bomber pilots were not even instructed to board their B-52s and get them safely into the air, according to Government officials.

The attack warning gave U.S. military commanders barely five minutes to react before the first Russian missiles—supposedly launched from submarines—were to hit targets, including all the SAC bomber bases, Government sources say. Yet it was not until a minute after these warheads were to have struck that Air Force technicians discovered the alert had been triggered by a computerized war game gone awry—a simulated attack tape had somehow gone out as the real thing. Nevertheless, neither President Carter nor Secretary Brown was informed.

Meanwhile, the sources say, the pilot and crew of Carter's E-4 jet command center (on runway alert at Andrews Air Base to allow a President to escape the initial holocaust and direct retaliation from the skies) dashed into the aircraft and took off without having heard from the President.

In June the reaction was much more vigorous—frighteningly so. According to Pentagon and other Government officials, here is what happened in those two cases:

Air Force officers deep underground at the North American Air Defense Command near Colorado Springs were routinely monitoring warning apparatus.

Suddenly, the fluorescent display screens connected to a "Nova" Data General computer flashed a warning: A large-scale Soviet missile attack of land-based and submarine missiles had just been launched.

The computer warned that Soviet missiles had been fired on a "depressed trajectory" from submarines positioned close to American shores. They would strike their targets here in as few as three minutes (the period of time it took to discover the error).

SAC was alerted and, at airfields across the United States, pilots and crews of 116 B-52 nuclear bombers on runway alert scrambled into their planes, gunned the engines, and began taxiing for takeoff. Nuclear submarine commanders also were alerted.

Inside underground launch centers near silos housing American ICBMs, missile launch officers strapped themselves into jolt-resistant swivel chairs, unlocked strongboxes, removed "attack verification codes" and launch keys, and inserted the keys into slots.

(When two keys ten feet apart are twisted within two seconds of each other, the warheads blast toward the Soviet Union.)

Shortly after the false alarm came to light, as unlikely a critic as Senator John Tower of Texas rejected the Pentagon's assurances that nothing dangerous had occurred. He predicted a Congressional investigation. The left wing of Britain's Labour Party expressed shock and called for a Parliamentary debate on the issue. And the Soviet Union accused the United States of harboring a "nuclear persecution complex."

Some critics are most concerned with what might happen if a false alarm were to recur in an even more tense East-West climate.

For instance, Bruce Blair of the Brookings Institution—an expert on nuclear attack warning systems and a former Air Force missile launch officer—suggested the following scenario:

The United States and the Soviets are on the brink of war because of a crisis in the Middle East, Africa, Western Europe, or all of the above. At this most inopportune time, the U.S. warning system decides to emit a false alarm of a Soviet atomic attack.

U.S. bombers take to the skies to avoid being blown to bits, and missiles are primed for quick launch.

Meanwhile, the Soviets, through their satellite sensors, detect that U.S. bombers have been launched. Fearful that submarine missiles and ICBMs are soon to follow, and that their own missiles will be destroyed in their silos, the Soviets unleash at least some of their warheads—not at our missile silos, which they fear would be empty, but at other military targets, quite possibly in heavily populated areas.

But, still fearing that U.S. missiles are the targets of a Russian first strike, we "retaliate" against the Soviet "retaliation" against the nonexistent American first strike, in order to save our own warheads from destruction. Apocalypse, close behind, obliterates the confusion.

Pentagon spokesman Thomas Ross refused to comment on such a scenario, but argued that a computer error could never prompt "retaliation" against a nonexistent attack. Attack warnings are verified or shown false through U.S. satellite sensors, he said.

But the problem is that the sensors, too, have been known to fail, occasionally reporting sunspots as missiles. Blair recalled a 1973 incident in which a computer misinterpreted sensor data about a Soviet test missile fired from a site near Iran. The computer predicted the missile would land in California, and sparked an alert. But the missile landed where it was aimed, in Kamchatka, Siberia.

In the above scenario for doomsday, the flashpoint was reached because each side was convinced its missiles were about to be destroyed on the ground. Indeed, the vulnerability of missiles has become almost an obsession with many in the military establishment because technological developments seem to have made the "hardened" missile silo obsolete.

But many of those more concerned with the vulnerability of the human race to accidental war than with the fate of hardened silos believe a grave danger is posed by U.S. strategy for deterring the Soviets from launching a first strike against American missiles.

The strategy, known as "launch-on-warning," has been embraced by Secretary Brown. He has warned the Soviets that the United States may well launch some or all of its warheads upon electronic detection that the Russians have launched theirs. General David Jones, chairman of the Joint Chiefs of Staff, assured the House Armed Services Committee last year that the United States has the capacity both to detect an attack and to retaliate before it arrives.

But given the demonstrated fallibility of electronic detection, the dangers of launch-on-warning are all too obvious.

Many are convinced that launch-on-warning may soon be transformed from an option in the American war plan into an imbedded doctrine. Partly as a result of the waning support for the MX missile concept of deploying missiles amid a cluster of empty silos for protection, the military establishment is seeking a "quick fix" for the problem of missile vulnerability.

Among the many objections to launch-on-warning is that, in effect, it relegates decision-making power to machines. Many defense analysts believe Soviet submarine missiles can hit their U.S. targets in as few as three minutes from first detection. ICBMs take fifteen or twenty minutes. In any event, there is little time for leaders to reflect on the course to take if they want to preserve the ability to launch on warning. So faulty information from machines could easily determine their decisions.

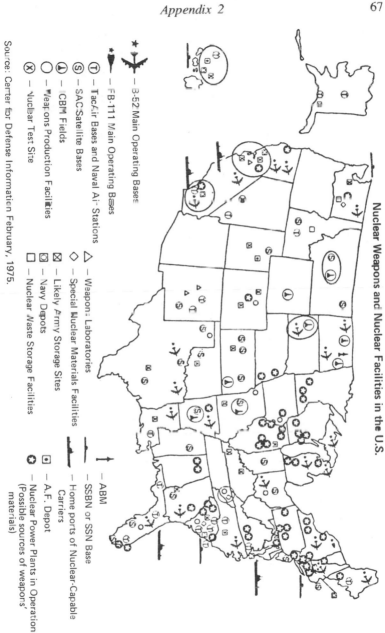

Nuclear Weapons and Nuclear Facilities in the U.S.

✈ — B-52 Main Operating Bases

➤ — FB-111 Main Operating Bases

Ⓣ — Tac Air Bases and Naval Air Stations

Ⓢ — SAC-Satellite Bases

Ⓐ — ICBM Fields

○ — Weapons Production Facilities

Ⓧ — Nuclear Test Site

△ — Weapons Laboratories

◇ — Special Nuclear Materials Facilities

⊠ — Likely Army Storage Sites

⊙ — Navy Depots

□ — Nuclear Waste Storage Facilities

✠ — ABM

➤ — SSBN or SSN Base

➤ — Home ports of Nuclear-Capable Carriers

⊡ — A.F. Depot

✿ — Nuclear Power Plants in Operation (Possible sources of weapons' materials)

Source: Center for Defense Information February, 1975.

We may be approaching the point where a computer chip could assume the role of Commander-in-Chief and decide whether to go to war.

Reprinted by permission from *The Progressive,* 408 West Gorham Street, Madison, Wis. 53703. © 1980, The Progressive, Inc.
Richard Thaxton is the penname of a Washington journalist.

GLOSSARY OF KEY NUCLEAR ARMS RACE TERMINOLOGY

Atomic Bomb—A nuclear weapon whose energy is derived from the fissioning or splitting the atom, releasing the heavy radioactive elements of uranium and plutonium.

Counterforce—The nuclear war strategy, also described as "first strike" or "countervailing strategy," in which attack missiles are targeted against the opponent's military forces, such as strategic airfields and land-based missiles, rather than against cities as in a deterrence strategy. Inasmuch as nuclear forces would be virtually invulnerable once launched, this strategy presupposes the first use of nuclear weapons rather than retaliatory strike.

On several occasions since development of the highly accurate multiple warhead technology, the U.S. government has announced the strategic option of using nuclear weapons in a first-strike capacity. (Secretary of Defense James Schlesinger, *New York Times,* 7/1/75; Secretary of Defense Harold Brown, *New York Times,* 8/6/80.) The Soviet Union is developing a nuclear counterforce strategy of its own in response to the determination of a U.S. counterforce policy.

Deterrence—A nuclear war strategy, also described as the "balance of terror," whereby from fear of massive retaliation, a potential aggressor refrains from using nuclear weapons. Since the early 1950s up until the institution of counterforce strategy in 1975, deterrence has characterized the relations between the United States and Soviet Union.

Fallout—Radioactive fission debris produced by above-ground (and some underground) nuclear explosions. It descends (or rises) to the surface of the earth, contaminating, in varying degrees, air, land, and water.

Hydrogen Bomb—A nuclear weapon, more specifically called a thermonuclear weapon, that generates its destructive power by a combination of atomic fusion and fission reactions. In contrast to the fission reaction, fusion, the primary reaction of the H-bomb, involves the joining together of atomic nuclei.

Intercontinental Ballistic Missile (ICBM)—A land-based rocket-propelled vehicle capable of delivering a warhead to intercontinental ranges up to 4,000 miles or more.

Kiloton—A measure of the yield of a nuclear weapon equivalent to 1,000 tons of TNT. The bomb dropped on Hiroshima in World War II had an approximate yield of 12.5 kilotons.

Limited Nuclear War—The deliberate, limited employment of tactical nuclear weapons against a specific military target or a populated area. This military concept of limitation presupposes that a nuclear conflict between two nations, or among several, would not necessarily escalate into a large-scale exchange of strategic nuclear weapons.

Megaton—A measure of the yield of a nuclear weapon equivalent to one million tons (or 1,000 kilotons) of TNT.

Multiple Warhead—A cluster of independently targetable nuclear weapons attached to a single launched missile. The MIRV, Multiple Independently Targeted Reentry Vehicle, is a highly accurate long-range nuclear warhead first developed by the U.S. in the early 1970s. The MARV, Maneuverable Reentry Vehicle, is an elaboration of the MIRV technology with an extreme target precision, longer range, and capacity for following the contour of the earth's terrain so as to avoid radar detection.

Mutual Assured Destruction (MAD)—The nuclear war strategy that has evolved from a credible deterrence strategy between the U.S. and the USSR since the late 1960s. It rests on a mutual understanding that either side can inflict massive destruction on the other in the event of a nuclear attack by one side. Often referred to as "MAD," it is theorized that this strategy maintains and enhances the deterrent effect between the superpowers.

National Security—A political and military term coined in the National Security Act of 1947. This act extended certain emergency powers to the President beyond those given in the U.S. Constitution. These powers include the prerogative to suspend civil liberties under certain circumstances as well as to undertake covert, normally illegal actions such as break-ins and wiretaps. Under this act, the United States has existed in an official state of national emergency since 1947. The development of nuclear weapons and the restriction of information about them have been accomplished largely without challenge because of the claims of national security.

Overkill—The nuclear deterrent concept of having an ability to destroy the entire population of an enemy nation several times over. Currently the U.S. and the USSR possess a nuclear weapons capability which can destroy the world's population fifteen times over.

Plutonium—A human-made, radioactive metallic element produced by the splitting of the uranium atom. Plutonium is used to make nuclear weapons and is produced by conventional nuclear power plants at the rate of several hundred pounds per plant each year. Only twenty pounds of plutonium is needed to produce an atomic bomb.

Plutonium, named after Pluto, the god of the underworld, is one of the most cancerous substances known and is so toxic that less than one-millionth of a gram can produce cancer. It retains its radioactivity for almost 250,000 years.

Proliferation—The spread to other nations of the capacity to produce nuclear weapons largely as a result of the exportation of nuclear energy technology and, more specifically, of gained access to plutonium.

Strategic Arms Limitation Talks (SALT)—A series of negotiations between the U.S. and the USSR which began in Helsinki in 1969, the aim of which is to set limits on strategic nuclear weapons. Since the beginnings of the SALT process however, both the U.S. and the USSR stockpiles have doubled and are predicted to triple by 1985. Despite the more than 6,000 official disarmament meetings between the superpowers, not a single weapon has yet been dismantled.

Strategic Nuclear Weapons—Long-range nuclear weapons with large kiloton or megaton yields carried on ICBMs, SLBMs and intercontinental bombers.

Submarine Launched Ballistic Missile (SLBM)—A rocket-propelled vehicle containing one or several nuclear warheads carried in, and launched from, a submarine.

Tactical Nuclear Weapons—Short-range weapons, such as the neutron bomb, intended for battlefield operations, particularly in a limited nuclear war scenario. Most U.S. tactical nuclear weapons are deployed in Western Europe and South Korea.

Triad—The three-part combination of land-based intercontinental ballistic missiles, airborne intercontinental bombers and cruise missiles, and submarine-launched ballistic missiles making up the deterrent forces of the U.S. and the USSR.

Uranium—The heaviest natural element; the basic raw material for nuclear power and nuclear weapons.

Yield—The explosive force of a nuclear weapon measured in kilotons or megatons.

APPENDIX 3

The Church on War and Peace

Christian Pacifism · 72

The Gospel and the Just War · 74

Denominational Statements on Peace and Nuclear
Disarmament · 76

Statements by Religious Groups on Peace and Nuclear
Disarmament · 80

Personal Statements on Peace and Nuclear Disarmament · 84

CHRISTIAN PACIFISM
Joseph Fahey

Much can be learned from the history of Christian pacifism in the quest for a human world order. Indeed, one might be so bold as to say that the pacifist experience of Christianity has never been so relevant as in our own century in which we must make a literally life-or-death decision concerning the human species. Martin Luther King's insight that today "the choice is between non-violence or nonexistence" is neither utopian nor optimistic—it is the product of a sober realism which tells us that we simply cannot continue on our present course.

It is time to challenge those who pursue the arms race to be "realistic." Their naïve assumption that a "balance of terror" will lead to a steady peace is backed neither by the tenets of morality, the basics of logic, nor the facts of history. Let us learn, then, from that Christian minority who chose life over death, nonviolence over violence, and resistance over submission.

In order to understand the long history of Christian pacifism one must, of course, examine the nonviolence of Jesus. It is quite clear that Jesus inherited the prophetic mandate for social justice and nonviolent reconciliation of enemies. He came to help "the blind see, the lame walk, the lepers (to be) cleansed, the deaf hear, the dead rise, the poor have the gospel preached to them" (Matt. 11:4–6). While Jesus' work was described principally in terms of justice (social justice, that is, since a completely individualistic ethic is impossible when talking about the needs of others), its method was the pursuit of nonviolence.

In the Sermon on the Mount Jesus blessed the peacemakers and said they should be called children of God (Matt. 5:9). He likewise counseled his followers, "You have heard the commandment, 'You shall love your country-man but hate your enemy.' My command to you is: love your enemies, pray for your persecutors. This will prove you are children of your heavenly Father . . ." (Matt. 5:43–45).

In one of his very last statements Jesus warned us that those who use the sword (violence) will perish by the sword (Matt. 26:54). He thus fulfilled his mission to be the Suffering Servant of God who would bring justice to his people by dying for them.

These passages present the main thrust of Jesus' attitude toward nonvio-lence. While isolated passages from the gospels have been used by some to justify violence, they have not swayed the opinions of contemporary Scripture scholars. In addition, these same scholars tell us that Jesus was put to death because of the social and political implications of his work. He was murdered by the Romans as if he were a revolutionary Zealot who threatened the estab-lished imperial order. Jesus' message was one of social justice and nonvio-lence—it attacked the very roots of the unjust and violent society in which he lived. He was, in essence, seeking to form a new global culture based on the priority of human needs and nonviolent love.

It is well known that for at least three centuries the early Christians followed

72

the pacifist example of Jesus. They were forbidden to kill enemies or join the army, and even those in the army had to resign when they were converted.

Four arguments are normally offered to explain the pacifism of early Christianity: the imminent Eschaton, aversion to Rome, idolatry, and the incompatibility between *agape* and war. One can conclude, however, that only the last reason was universally approved by the early Fathers of the Church and Christians in general. This was because the Christian word for love—*agape*— meant selfless concern for others, even one's enemies. It was thus inconceivable to the early Christians that one could fulfill Jesus' command to love one's enemy while at the same time preparing to kill that person.

Clearly, the early Christians believed that because they were followers of Jesus they could not kill. The following quotes are representative:

Christ in disarming Peter ungirt every soldier.

—Tertullian

It is not right for us either to see or hear a man being killed.
　　　　　　　　　　　　　　—Minucius Felix

God did not deem it becoming to his own divine legislation to allow the killing of any man whatsoever.

—Origen

We who were filled with war and mutual slaughter and every wickedness have each of us in all the world changed our weapons of war . . . swords into plows and spears into agricultural instruments . . . We who formerly murdered one another now not only do not lie or deceive our judges, we gladly die confessing Christ.

—Justin Martyr

In A.D. 295 a North African named Maximilian was beheaded because he refused to serve in the Roman army. He believed that Christians must conscientiously refuse military service. During his trial he stated: "My arms are with the Lord. I cannot fight for any earthly consideration. I am now a Christian . . . and it is unlawful to do evil."

The early Christians saw themselves as global citizens whose mission was to continue the witness of Jesus in "comforting the afflicted and afflicting the comfortable" by being pacifists (peacemakers) in his name. One could argue that the Christian community was never so strong as when it was weak and never so powerful as when it was powerless. We must remember that the nonviolent witness of the early Christians conquered the most powerful empire then existent in the world. Those who argue that, from a historical viewpoint, nonviolence has not worked must explain how Christians overcame the Roman Empire without armies or violence.

But, alas, the victory was not permanent, for by the fourth and fifth centuries thinkers such as Ambrose and Augustine had abandoned any hope for the Kingdom in this life and had come to accept the doctrine of the "just war." There is strong evidence to indicate that a major reason why many Christians accepted the use of violence to defend the Roman Empire was the growing fusion between Rome and Christianity. Many came to believe that the *Pax Christiana* and the *Pax Romana* were joint works of God.

This fusion between Christianity and nationalism led to the acceptance of violence as an instrument of national (Christian) policy. The Church has never been the same since. The "just war" in the fifth century led to the Crusades in the eleventh century. By that time nonviolence not only was not accepted by the Christian leadership, it was considered sinful and a sign of weakness.

But pacifism has always survived in Christianity. Religious orders of men and women carefully preserved the nonviolent witness of the early Church. People such as Benedict (d.c. 547, Italy), Francis (1182?–1226, Italy), Clare (1193?–1253, Italy), Ignatius Loyola (1491–1556, Spain), Erasmus (1466–1536, Holland), Thomas More (1478–1535, England), and the numerous orders of religious women have given us an unending witness of nonviolent service which would take volumes to fill. We owe them much.

The Protestant churches have given no less dramatic testimony. The most outstanding witnesses have been the Quakers, the Anabaptists (now the Mennonites and the Hutterites) and the Brethren. These people have often influenced society in far greater proportion than their numbers and persevered in pacifism through persecution, war, and social rejection.

In our own time a remarkable phenomenon seems to be taking place. Almost all Christian churches seem to be returning (in various degrees) to the pacifism of early Christianity. Undoubtedly new biblical and theological scholarship is spurring this movement. In addition, however, many are coming to realize that unless we adopt a more pacifist witness we simply will not survive. In short, be it from practical necessity or from biblical and historical insight, many more Christians are coming to see war and violence, including institutional violence, as the central blasphemy of our age.

We are called to be one race—a human race—and are challenged to create a truly human world order. It is within our power but is it within our vision? The discovery of the long history of Christian pacifism should remind us that so many others have not lost that vision. We are spiritual descendents of parents who have longed for a truly human world. We cannot fail them.

Joseph J. Fahey is former director of the Peace Studies Institute at Manhattan College and is the author of *Peace, War, and the Christian Conscience,* and *Reinhold Niebuhr on Human Nature and World Peace.*

THE GOSPEL AND THE JUST WAR
Richard T. McSorley, S.J.

Does war, does the killing of other human beings, the massive killing such as that which goes on in war, ever have the approval of the gospel? The answer is clearly: "No." There are different schools of interpretation of the gospel, but none of them denies that the gospel is itself pacifist (leaving aside tradition for a moment). And in being essentially pacifistic it clearly illustrates this point of view with the life and death of Jesus himself. He had all power and did not use it to inflict suffering, but rather taught a way of salvation by accepting suffering. How, then, did Christians ever come to accept war?

They came to accept it through the set of circumstances which affected them in the fourth century. When Augustine observed the political situation, he saw a Christian church which had fought the Roman state and now was allied with it. Seeing a threat to the whole church from the barbarians, he urged Christians to join the army; but this position he limited and justified in a set of conditions he established, now known as the "Just War Theory."

These conditions stated, approximately, that the gospel does say "Thou shalt not kill" and "Love thy neighbor," but that under certain rigorous conditions the killing that goes on in war is not always a violation of the gospel, but rather is an *exception*.

The conditions are:

   that war is waged only as a last resort;
   that war is waged under the authority of a ruler;
   that war is conducted in a just manner, so that there is no wanton killing;
   that the evil allowed is proportionate to the good which is being sought;
   that the innocent are protected;
   that the intention is good.

All of these conditions must be present *all* the time in *every* war. And if this is true all the time, Augustine says, then war is not a violation of the Gospel, but an act of mercy and an act of love in the reparation of justice.

What is wrong with this theory? In the nuclear age the theory is outmoded by technology, just as other things in our lives are outmoded by technology. A common argument to show that the just war theory is no good is simply to show that it has never worked. We have never yet had a war in history which has been condemned by society at large at the time as a violation of the just war theory; nor has any such war been condemned retroactively. Not even the German bishops condemned the wars of Hitler on the basis of any kind of Christian theory. Cardinal Alfrink says that one of the weaknesses of the theory is that it allows each nation to decide for itself—each nation remains the judge in its own case.

The just war theory also presupposes what was never really true: that one can be a just killer, or, to leave out the word *killer,* that one side is just and the other unjust. The just war theory supposes that some killing is allowable. This is illustrated in Paul Ramsey's book on the limits of nuclear war, which he subtitles, *How Shall War Be Conducted?* It omits the basic question: "Is any war just?" The just war theory, by its very name, allows that some war *is* just. It also presupposes that the head of state is a Christian or a follower of the just war theory. What good does this do when a Hitler is the head of state?

It impresses me, above all, that the just war theory uses the arguments of Aristotle, Cicero, and Plato. Christ's love ethic and the example of his life have nothing to do with this use of philosophical argumentation. Christ might as well not have come if our arguments about the main moral problem today—

human survival in the nuclear age—are going to ignore Christ's example and his teaching.

Reprinted from *U. S. Catholic* magazine, 221 West Madison Street, Chicago, Ill. 60606.

Richard McSorley, S. J., teaches peace theology at Georgetown University, and is the author of *Kill? For Peace?* and *New Testament Basis of Peacemaking*.

DENOMINATIONAL STATEMENTS ON PEACE AND NUCLEAR DISARMAMENT

Church of the Brethren

The Church of the Brethren, since its beginning in 1708, has repeatedly declared its position against war. Our understanding of the life and teachings of Christ as revealed in the New Testament led our Annual Conference to state in 1785 that we should not "submit to the higher powers so as to make ourselves their instruments to shed human blood." In 1918, at our Annual Conference, we stated that "we believe that war or any participation in war is wrong and incompatible with the spirit, example and teachings of Jesus Christ." Again in 1934 our Annual Conference resolved that all war is sin. We, therefore, cannot encourage, engage in, or willingly profit from armed conflict at home or abroad. We cannot, in the event of war, accept military service or support the military machine in any capacity . . . We call upon all of our members, congregations, institutions, and boards to study seriously the problem of paying taxes for war purposes and investing in those government bonds which support war. We further call upon them to act in response to their study, to the leading of conscience, and to their understanding of the Christian faith. To all we pledge to maintain our continuing ministry of fellowship and spiritual concern.

Statements on War and Taxes approved by the 1968 Annual Conference.

Episcopal Church

In the face of the mounting incidence of violence today and its acceptance as a normal element in human affairs, we condemn the subjection, intimidation, and manipulation of people by the use of violence and the threat of violence and call Christian people everywhere:

—to reexamine as a matter of urgency their own attitude toward, and their complicity with, violence in its many forms;
—to engage themselves in nonviolent action for justice and peace and to support others so engaged, recognizing that such action will be controversial and may be personally very costly;

—to commit themselves to informed, disciplined prayer not only for all victims of violence, especially for those who suffer their obedience to the Man of the Cross, but also for those who inflict violence on others; to protest in whatever way possible the escalation of the sale of armaments of war by the producing nations to the developing and dependent nations, and to support with every effort all international proposals and conferences designed to place limitations on, or arrange reductions in, the armaments of war of the nations of the world.

Lambeth Conference 1978, "War and Violence," Resolution No. 5.

Lutheran Church

It is clearly time for a rethinking of the meaning of national security. In view of the overkill capacity now possessed by the superpowers, national security can no longer be defined in terms of either nuclear superiority or even nuclear stalemate. The common threat which such weapons hold for all humanity teaches that their continued development can only undermine security. . . .

This effort (to bring about arms control) should be intensified, should become increasingly multinational in character, and should include all weapons of mass destruction. In the meantime, the United States should be encouraged to undertake such unilateral initiatives as may contribute to a climate more hospitable to the limitation of arms . . . Peace will be established not through the suppression of human aspirations but rather through the provision of structures within which they can flourish.

From Lutheran Church in America "Social Statement in World Community," adopted in 1970.

Mennonite and Brethren in Christ Churches

At this midpoint of the twentieth century, at a critical time in a generation marked by widespread and disastrous wars and shadowed by the threat of still more ruinous warfare, this conference of delegated representatives from the Mennonite and Brethren in Christ Churches of the United States and Canada unites in a renewed declaration of faith in Jesus Christ, the Prince of Peace, in His Gospel, and in His power to redeem and transform in life and in human society all those who receive him as Savior and Lord and are thus born anew by the Spirit of God. It is our faith that Christ has established in His Church a universal community within which the fullness of Christ's reign must be practiced, into which the redeemed must be brought, and from which must go out into all human society the saving and healing ministry of the Gospel. . . .

We cannot therefore participate in military service of any form. We cannot have any part in financing war operations. We cannot knowingly participate in the manufacture of weapons of war. We cannot take part in any program for war.

Statement of Winona Lake Conference of Mennonites and Brethren in Christ Churches, 1950. Since 1950 this statement has been reaffirmed by the Mennonite Central Committee Peace Section as well as other individual church bodies.

The Religious Society of Friends (Quakers)

We feel bound explicitly to avow our unshaken persuasion that all war is utterly incompatible with plain precepts of our divine Lord and Lawgiver, and the whole spirit of His Gospel, and that no plea of necessity or policy, however urgent or peculiar, can avail to release either individuals or nations from the paramount allegiance which they owe to Him who has said, "Love your enemies."

Friends are urged:

—to avoid engaging in any trade, business, or profession directly contributing to the military system;
—to consider carefully the implication of paying those taxes, a major portion of which goes for military purposes.

Statement from "Declaration of Faith" issued by the Richmond Conference of Friends.

In humility and repentance for past failures, we call upon all Friends to renew the springs and sources of spiritual power in our meetings for worship; to examine our possessions, to see if there be any seed of war in them; and to live heroically in that life and power that takes away the occasion of all wars and strife.

Statement of a Conference of All American Friends in Richmond, Indiana, 1948. Reaffirmed by the Friends Coordinating Committee on Peace, and by a number of Yearly Meetings, 1968.

Roman Catholic Church

Any act of war aimed indiscriminately at the destruction of entire cities and their inhabitants, is a crime against God and humanity itself which must be condemned firmly and without hesitation.

(Vatican II)

The armaments race is to be condemned unreservedly. It is a danger . . . an injustice . . . a mistake . . . a folly. It is an act of aggression which amounts to a crime, for even when they are not used, by their cost alone, armaments kill the poor by causing them to starve.

(Holy See Statement on Disarmament, issued to the United Nations on May 7, 1976.)

As possessors of a vast nuclear arsenal, we must be aware that not only is it wrong to attack civilian populations, but it is also wrong to threaten to attack them as part of a strategy of deterrence.

Taken from the pastoral letter, *To Live in Christ Jesus,* issued by the National Conference of Catholic Bishops, November 1976.

Southern Baptist Convention

We confess we have not pursued peace with full Christian commitment. We urge Washington representatives to move in imaginative ways to seek mutual agreements with other nations to stop the arms race . . . We call for a shift of funds from nuclear weapons to basic human needs.

A resolution calling for multilateral arms control, 133rd Annual Convention, June 10, 1978.

United Church of Christ (UCC)

We are called by the life, death, and resurrection of Jesus Christ to a ministry of reconciliation, for he is our peace who has made us one (Ephesians 2); . . .

There is a threat to the whole human family, in the spreading danger of nuclear war; and as Christians we have a particular responsibility to resist the power of this evil; . . .

Billions are being spent for arms, while people's basic needs such as food, housing, health care, and education are underfunded, that to be able to kill and be killed many times over in the name of defense is an evil waste of world resources.

From The 12th General Synod of the United Church of Christ, Pronouncement on "Reversing the Arms Race," 1979.

United Methodist Church

If humanity is to move out of this period of futility and constant peril, the search for new weapons systems must be halted through comprehensive international agreements. Moreover, disarmament negotiations should include all nations with substantial armaments systems. The vast stockpiles of nuclear bombs and conventional weapons must be dismantled under international supervision, and the resources being used for arms diverted to programs designed to affirm life rather than destroying it.

From "The United Methodist Church and Peace," adopted by the 1976 General Conference in Portland, Oregon.

United Presbyterian Church in the U.S.A.

Ominous clouds hang over human history. There are frightening risks in the continuing arms race and looming conflicts over diminishing energy resources as centers of power struggle for control. Our fear for safety has led us to take life; and now we are in danger of taking our own lives as well. . . .

But we believe that these times, so full of peril and tragedy for the human family, present a special call for obedience to our Lord, the Prince of Peace. The Spirit is calling us to life out of death . . . We are at a turning point. We are faced with the decision either to serve the Rule of God, or to side with the powers of death through our complacency and silence. . . .

We know that peace cannot be achieved simply by ending the arms race, unless there is economic and political justice in the human family. Peace is the intended order of the world with life abundant for all God's children. Peacemaking is the calling of the Christian Church, for Christ is our peace who has made us one through his body on the cross.

Taken from the 192nd General Assembly Report, "Peacemaking: The Believers' Calling," 1980.

STATEMENTS BY RELIGIOUS GROUPS ON PEACE AND NUCLEAR DISARMAMENT

We are convinced that the arms race cannot be won; it can only be lost. All of us have long been aware of the nuclear terror. Many have accepted it as an inescapable part of our contemporary world. Numerous voices in the church have been raised against it in both our countries. Our experience in this consultation now compels us to cry out against it with one voice. The existence of forces having the capacity to devastate our planet not once or twice, but many times, is absurd and cannot be tolerated. It must be confronted and overcome in the name of the Christ who lives and reigns forever.

We express profound concern about the danger of a precarious balancing of humanity on the brink of nuclear catastrophe. We know that still more terrible weapons are being developed which can only lead to greater fear and suspicion and thus to a still more feverish arms race. Against this we say with one voice—No. In the name of God—No . . .

Thus the Lord has set before us again life and death, blessing and curse: Therefore choose life that you and your descendants may live.

From *Choose Life,* joint statement of the representatives of the churches of the USSR and the U.S. meeting in Geneva in a consultation on disarmament on March 27–29, 1979.

Sojourners Peace Ministry

We are soberly reminded of God's command, "You shall have no other gods before me." But we have fallen away from God by joining our fellow citizens in succumbing to the idolatry of military might and power. To plan nuclear war assumes that tens of millions will die justifiably in the name of national security. This exalts the nation above all else, including the survival of humanity.

Our professed allegiance to Christ and his Kingdom rings hollow when we accept military policies of indiscriminate mass destruction, placing us in direct opposition to Christ's unequivocal instruction to love our enemies, do good to those who hate us, bless those who curse us, and pray for those who persecute us . . .

Our primary allegiance to Jesus Christ and his Kingdom commits us to total abolition of nuclear weapons. There can be no qualifying or conditioning word. We, the signers of this declaration, commit ourselves to noncooperation with our country's preparations for nuclear war. On all levels—research, development, testing, production, deployment, and actual use of nuclear weapons—we commit ourselves to resist in the name of Jesus Christ.

From *A Call to Faithfulness,* circulated by the Sojourner Peace Ministry in Washington, D.C., and signed by over 200 religious leaders from around the country.

World Council of Churches

We scientists, engineers, theologians, and members of Christian churches from all parts of the world . . . acknowledge with penitence the part played by science in the development of weapons of mass destruction and the failure of the churches to oppose it, and now plead with the nations of the world for the reduction and eventual abolition of such weapons.

From *Resolution on Disarmament: Science of Peace,* World Council of Churches, Conference on Faith, Science and the Future, July 12—24, 1979. Cambridge, Massachusetts.

National Council of Churches

As part of a people gripped by the anguish that their nation and the world are steadily moving toward war, it is time for the churches to cry "Enough"! With the United States and the Soviet Union possessing destructive power which threatens God's creative work on earth, we who participate in the body of our incarnate Lord reject the blasphemy of nuclear destruction of those for whom Christ died.

We urge the official bodies of our constituent communions to call upon the U.S. government and to invite the government of the Soviet Union to negotiate a moratorium on all further testing, production, and deploying of nuclear weapons and their launchers.

Popular sentiment is for more armament. We must find a way to help popular sentiment change. Therefore it is the recommendation of this Consultation that the member denominations of the NCC provide the local faith communities with the resources, staff support, and encouragement that will enable them to be a faithful support group for the work of peace, justice, and disarmament. The work of the churches in disarmament should be aimed at fostering the efforts of local faith communities in peace and justice and in giving every member a chance to take part in this work.

From the NCC Disarmament Consultation held in Pittsburgh, Pa., April 29 through May 1, 1980.

Fellowship of Reconciliation

The FOR is committed to "work to abolish war and create a community of concern transcending all national boundaries and selfish interests; as an integral part of that commitment we refuse to participate personally in any war, or to give any sanction we can withhold from physical, moral, or psychological preparation for war.''

From the Fellowship of Reconciliation (FOR), a worldwide ecumenical pacifist peace organization founded in 1914.

Mobilization for Survival

We believe that a Nuclear Moratorium on the production and use of nuclear weapons and reactors is a necessary expression of our hope that a human future is still possible.

What does God require of us in the face of such threats to all of our children? The failure of the German churches under Hitler to speak out is a burning reminder for all believers as we confront the prospects of the final holocaust, which are foreshadowed by the present nuclear society.

Can we stand by silent in the face of a military strategy based on the readiness to engage in the mass murder of millions of people, most of them civilians, many of them children, all held hostage by nuclear weapons?

Can we accept the enormous slander that the wish to destroy each other is so deep inside ''them'' and ''us'' that only the arms race can serve as a deterrent?

Can we passively continue to accept the daily radioactive assault on our children's health, safety, and future?

In the name of the Spirit of Life, we call on all people of goodwill to demand that our government initiate an immediate nuclear moratorium as an example to other nations and as a first step to human survival:

—Stop the testing, research, development, and production of nuclear
    weapons.
—Pledge never to use nuclear weapons in a first strike.
—Halt the construction, operation, and export of nuclear reactors.
—Cease the transport of nuclear materials except those clearly intended
    to protect health.
—Ban mining, milling, processing, and transport of uranium.

In the name of the Spirit called Justice, we insist:

—That the riches of the earth be used to rebuild our cities and to feed,
    clothe, house, teach, and heal our children, instead of for weapons of
    destruction;
—That the funds now used for nuclear power be used to develop safe
    and clean sources of energy, which will be gentle with the earth and
    its children;
—That the economic conversion of military and nuclear power industries
    and the retraining of their workers be undertaken ''because it is un-
    thinkable that no other work can be found for hundreds of thousands
    of workers than the production of instruments of death.'' (Paul VI)

A call for a nuclear moratorium is a radical expression of our hope that there is still time for a deep spiritual conversion from our present values to something new. Only through this inner transformation, this ''change in our attitudes toward one another as well as our concept of the future'' (Einstein) can an authentic and lasting outer transformation take place. A nuclear moratorium will give us time to repair the damage caused by the nuclear build-up. It will give us time to work toward complete disarmament, toward a nuclear-free future and toward lasting social justice for all people.

The words of Jesus offer us the faith and hope of children as a source of inspiration for the difficult task ahead: "Whoever does not accept the Kingdom of God like a child will never enter it." (Mark 10:15)

From the *Religious Call for a Nuclear Moratorium* produced by the Religious Task Force of the Mobilization for Survival, 1979 (The International Year of the Child).

Life or Oblivion

A Call from the Hibakusha of Hiroshima and Nagasaki to the Hibakusha of the World, August 2, 1977.

Women and men, young people and children of the world, unite! You have nothing to lose but the chains that bind you to the increasing armaments and war. Unless you can break those chains, we may lose our jobs, our homes, our schools, our playgrounds, our lives, our culture, our civilization, our world.

We are all survivors of the Hiroshima and Nagasaki bombs. *We* are all survivors of the Hiroshima and Nagasaki bombs. We also are *hibakusha,* as the survivors of those cities call themselves. Although we did not experience the blast and the burns, we all carry in our bodies man-made radioactivity that would never have been there but for the nuclear explosions which have followed since 1945. Those bombs killed 300,000 people, women, men, young people, children, babies, animals, birds, and fish—every form of life. They killed many more even of those gallant and desperate people who came to the cities afterward looking for relatives or to give their help.

We survived those bombs, but we are threatened now by a million bombs more powerful than the bombs which destroyed Hiroshima and Nagasaki, as we are threatened by the prospect of neutron bombs, of cruise missiles and the development of more accurate strategic weapons.

Not only pacifists and idealists warn us of this mortal danger, but the leaders of the nations, Presidents and Prime Ministers, Ministers of Defense and military men. And more important is the solemn warning from scientists, some of whom helped to create the bombs and the missile systems that we are facing now.

The scientists warn us that we are in danger of destroying our civilizations and even human life itself. If these weapons are ever used—and scientists tell us that there is an increasing probability that they will be used—if they are ever used, unless we can reverse the present trends, the earth would become as barren and sterile as the moon. If we end the arms race we can rebuild decaying cities, we can make the homes, the work, the schools, the hospitals that every nation needs. We can wipe out preventable disease. We can teach every person in the world to read and write, and open to them the world of culture. We can make life happy and noble for all people everywhere.

If we drift on as we are drifting now, we may sleepwalk into the final catastrophe. Then the human race will perish, and no human voice will ever speak again.

The lessons of Hiroshima and Nagasaki may yet save humankind—if we are willing now to learn those lessons. If we learn them we must act without delay. Time is short.

Hibakusha of the world unite. We are the people of a glorious future yet to be.

PERSONAL STATEMENTS ON PEACE AND NUCLEAR DISARMAMENT

Albert Einstein

On the day the bomb was dropped on Hiroshima, on that day the American people assumed responsibility before the eyes of the world for the release of the most revolutionary force since the discovery of fire. Each of us, whether as scientists who made the bomb possible and/or as citizens of the nations that applied the knowledge, stands accountable for the use we made and make of this tremendous new force. To our generation has come the possibility of making the most fateful decision in the recorded history of the human race. I believe that human beings capable of restraint, reason, and courage, will choose the path of peace. Each of us has it in our power today to act for peace.

(From Albert Einstein, Aug. 6, 1946, 1st Commemoration of the Bombing of Hiroshima.)

Mohandas K. Gandhi

I regard the employment of the atomic bomb for the wholesale destruction of men, women, and children as the most diabolical use of science. Nonviolence is the only thing the atom bomb cannot destroy . . . Unless now the worlds adopts nonviolence, it will spell certain suicide for humanity.

(From Mohandas K. Gandhi, *Nonviolence in Peace and War*.)

Dorothy Day

All our talks about peace and the weapons of the spirit are meaningless unless we try in every way to embrace voluntary poverty and not work in any position, any job that contributes to war, nor to take any job whose pay comes from the fear of war, of the atom bomb.

(Dorothy Day, from *On Pilgrimage*.)

Martin Luther King

If we assume that humankind has a right to survive then we must find an alternative to war and destruction. In a day when sputniks dash through outer space and guided ballistic missiles are carving highways of death through the stratosphere, nobody can win a war. The choice today is no longer between violence and nonviolence. It is either nonviolence or nonexistence.

I am convinced that the Church cannot remain silent while humankind faces the threat of being plunged into the abyss of nuclear annihilation. If the Church is to remain true to its mission it must call for an end to the arms race.

(Martin Luther King, Jr., "Pilgrimage to Nonviolence" in his book, *Strength to Love*.)

Sarah Hutchinson

A thousand years ago the young men buried their fathers, during wartime the fathers buried the young men; now with nuclear technology we are burying the children of the future.

(Sarah Hutchinson, Cherokee teacher.)

Mother Teresa

We believe what Jesus has said: "I was hungry; I was naked; I was homeless; I was unwanted, unloved, uncared for—and you did it to me." I believe that we are not real social workers. We may be doing social work in the eyes of the people, but we are really contemplatives in the heart of the world. For we are touching the body of Christ twenty-four hours a day. We have twenty-four hours in this presence, and so do you and I. You too must try to bring that presence of God in your family, for the family that prays together stays together. And I think that we in our family, we don't need bombs and guns to destroy, to bring peace—just get together, love one another, bring that peace, that joy, that strength to each other in our homes. And we will be able to overcome all the evil that is in the world. There is so much suffering, so much hatred, so much misery; and we with our prayer, with our sacrifice, are beginning at home. Love begins at home, and it is not how much we do, but how much love we put in the action that we do.

(Mother Teresa of Calcutta in her Nobel Peace Prize acceptance speech in Stockholm, Sweden, December 11, 1979)

James Douglass

Faith is believing that there is hope for our world. Despair is denying that our nuclear war systems can be stopped or changed. Faith is a commitment to the world's transformation through God to a Kingdom of justice and peace. Faith's denial is mindlessness and hopelessness—yours and mine—in the face of the Pentagon and its corporations, a despair whose consequences for the world would have no parallel in history. Never before has our despair at changing institutions threatened the extinction of all life on earth. Faith is belief in a reality, and a transformation through which it is possible for us to live deeply enough to choose new life rather than nuclear death. A lived faith will stop the bomb.

We need to join in a community committed to that nonviolent life-force which is the power of the powerless. We need to test the truth by betting our lives on it in the world. If a community can experiment deeply enough in a nonviolent life-force the power of the Pentagon will crumble.

(James Douglass, author and peace activist, from his article, "Living at the End of the World" which appeared in *Fellowship* magazine, January/February 1979.)

A Child's Memory of Nagasaki

"Does anyone really believe," asks one senator, "that the United States and Russia could have a controlled nuclear exchange, silo to silo, and then sit down at the peace table and call it off?" It is most unlikely. But to contemplate nuclear war, heads of state must close out all thoughts of the human cost. They need to be reminded by someone who lived through it. Fujio Tsujimoto survived the bombing of Nagasaki. He was six years old when his world fell apart. He wrote about it several years later. We do not know where he is now.

I believe I escaped death when the atom bomb fell on Nagasaki only because I happened to be in the air raid shelter on the boundary of our Yamazato grade school playground.

Of the many people who were in the school that day, only three of us escaped with our lives: my grandmother, my school comrade Tagawa, and I.

The sirens howled loudly. The old people and the children of Ueno Street sought shelter as usual in the air raid basement. Inside the school the air raid watch and the first aid people took their places. The wardens, the doctors, and many other grown-ups hurried past. Our teacher also took part in the preparations.

Since the airplanes were not sighted, the all-clear signal was sounded. Every one left the cellar and went out into the air. We children tumbled out onto the playground making a lot of noise. The men and women also came over to rest themselves. There was a great crowd of people on the playground . . .

Suddenly there was a loud explosion. The other children were fooling and quarreling too loud to hear it, but I grasped Grandmother by the hand and ran with her toward the air-raid shelter.

"Enemy fliers, enemy fliers," a warden shouted. Horrified, the rest of the people stormed wildly toward the entrance of the cellar. Grandmother and I, who were at the front of the crowd, ran into the farthest corner.

There was a dazzling glare. A powerful gust of wind smashed me against the cellar wall. After some time I looked out of the cellar. Everywhere people lay thickly on top of each other, dead; only here and there one moved a leg or another raised an arm. Those who could still move crawled on all fours toward us in the cellar, which gradually became filled with wounded.

The row houses in the vicinity of the school were burning brightly. Our house too burned in a big blaze.

My brother and my little sisters had come into the shelter too late. They were badly burned. They sat beside me and cried. Grandmother took the rosary from her kimono and prayed.

I sat down at the entrance of the shelter and looked around, yearning for Father and Mother. Half an hour later my mother did come. Her whole body was bloody. Mother had been surprised by the attack while she was preparing dinner. I'll never forget the joy I felt when I threw myself upon my mother. Full of worry we waited for Father. He had gone away in the morning on warden duty.

The people who were still alive died one after another. They groaned in pain. The next day my young sisters died, and also mother, our beloved mother. Then my brother. I believed that I also would die. Everyone that was with us in the cellar died. Grandmother and I, however, had been the deepest into the shelter. The blast had not reached us. Therefore we remained alive, just we two.

Day after day we searched in vain among the many dead for my father.

Only a few remained alive. These carried a lot of wood onto the playground and burned the corpses. My brother was burned there too. Before my eyes my mother became ashes.

Grandmother said to me that when I come to Heaven I will see my mother again. Yes, but Grandmother is already old. She will soon go to Heaven. But I, I am only a child and must live many, many years before I can be united with Mother, whom I love more than anything; before I can again play with my brother and talk with my small sisters.

I am now attending the Yamazato grade school once more. I am now in fourth grade. The playground is cleaned up now and many of my school friends play there. Those children know nothing about the fact that many, many of their comrades died and were burned to ashes here. Even I run happily around the playground with my companions. But often and unexpectedly images of that horrible day leap up before me.

Then I throw myself down on the piece of earth where my mother was burned. My fingers tear the ground. If one bores deeper with a bamboo stick black ashes and charcoal come to the surface. When I look directly at the earth suddenly the face of my mother is visible in it. I rage when I see my school friends walk on that ground.

Grandmother goes every morning to Mass in the church. She prays with the rosary. "All is the will of God," she says to me. I wish I had such a pure heart as Grandmother's.

Reprinted from *Fellowship*, August 1980. Available from Fellowship Publications, Box 271, Nyack, N.Y. 10960.

APPENDIX 4

Human and Economic Costs
of the Nuclear Arms Race

Waking America up to the Nuclear Nightmare · 90

The Arms Race or the Human Race · 93

Do You Know What Your Tax Dollar Buys? · 96

Converting from Military to Peace Production · 97

WAKING AMERICA UP TO THE NUCLEAR NIGHTMARE

An interview with Dr. Helen Caldicott conducted in February 1979 by Rob Okun, editor of *New Roots* magazine.

Australian-born and -educated, Dr. Helen Caldicott has practiced pediatrics at Boston Children's Hospital Medical Center. An environmental activist since 1971, she virtually single-handedly educated and inspired the Australian public to protest—and to bring to a halt—French atmospheric testing in the South Pacific. Married and the mother of three children, Dr. Caldicott has become a leading critic of the development of nuclear weapons and nuclear energy, and is the author of *Nuclear Madness: What You Can Do.*

Q: Why do you say there are only two years before the arms race will be out of control?

A: There are two reasons. Within two years the technologists at the Pentagon will have finished developing a system called "launch-on-warning." That means when the computer in our reconnaissance satellite detects something in Russia—maybe it's a missile going off, maybe it's an accident, maybe it's nothing—it sends a message back to all the missiles in America which go off within *three minutes. And there's no human input!* No human being will be able to stop it.

Then there are the Cruise missiles. They are small strategic weapons, about 10 to 20 feet long. Because they're so small they can be easily hidden and can't be counted. Up to now Russia and America could count each other's strategic weapons by satellite. That's why we got SALT II— you don't have to trust each other. Without the Cruise, America and Russia—for the first time—are essentially equivalent. The Cruise missile means the end of any possibility for detente, the end of the SALT talks. Was there a national debate about this very important decision? Was it discussed in Congress and the Senate? No!

Q: We hear more talk about the energy crisis than the threat of nuclear war. Are the American people aware of how grave the situation is?

A: Not yet. Most of America is sound asleep. Do you know we nearly had a nuclear war on November 9, 1979? A fellow in the Pentagon plugged a war games tape into a supposedly failsafe computer and the computer took it for real. All the American early warning systems around the world went on alert for six minutes. Three squadrons of planes took off armed with nuclear weapons. At the seventh minute the Presidential 747 command post was readied for take-off. (They couldn't find the President. He was to be notified at the seventh minute.) If in 20 minutes it hadn't been stopped, we wouldn't be here right now. Remember 20 minutes is currently the time limit for a retaliatory nuclear attack. There would have been a full-scale nuclear war and it was *back page* in the *New York Times!* But it was front-page headlines in the London *Guardian!* The rest of the world is petrified! This country is a sleeping giant! It is totally unaware of the incredible power it holds and the magnitude of destruction inherent in its arsenals.

Q: Many nuclear critics believe that most of the media is so caught up in listening to the doublespeak of the Defense Department and the Department of Energy that they regularly miss opportunities to break major stories. Why do you think they underplayed such a gripping, nearly catastrophic story?

A: It's typical. I really don't think they understand the gravity of the issue. Nuclear war has little to do with a post-Three Mile Island consciousness and it is something they don't want to think about. Were they told to hush it up by the Pentagon? I don't know. The rest of the world is more awake than America because they *know* what war is. That's why it made the front page overseas. Modern America has never suffered war on its own soil.

Q: What would be the probable scenario of a nuclear war?

A: If the button is pressed in Russia or America, the weapons go out into space and reenter the earth's atmosphere at 20 times the speed of sound. And, they're accurately on target. Meanwhile, the satellite from the other country has detected the attack and the button is pressed in that country. So a nuclear war takes about one to two hours to complete. If you live in a targeted area and you do manage to get into a fallout shelter, you won't survive because the firestorms will be so huge. One 20-metaton bomb (20 million tons of TNT equivalent) will create a firestorm of 3,000 square miles. The fire will use up all the oxygen in the air, so if you're in a shelter, you'll asphyxiate. One 20-megaton bomb would literally vaporize everything in Boston up to Route 128, except reinforced concrete buildings.

Q: Are you saying that no one will survive all-out nuclear war?

A: Well, very possibly. And you might not want to survive. If you're in a rural area and you do hear the sirens and you get to a shelter in time, you can't come up for two weeks because short-lived radioactive isotopes are so intensely radioactive that you'd die. When you do come out in two weeks, from a psychiatric point of view, you'll be numb with grief, possibly psychotic. Certainly there will be no doctors left, or hospitals, because they're targeted. There will be no food. The water will be intensely radioactive. It's possible that the destruction of the ozone layer will be so intense that you won't be able to stay out in the sun for more than three minutes before you'd develop third-degree sunburn. That means the earth will be a parched, scorched planet. If you survive you must live underground to escape the fallout. And you'd probably get leukemia in five years.

The civil defense manual written by the Pentagon says to very quickly bury the millions of dead, decaying bodies before disease becomes rampant. In a radioactive environment the bacteria and viruses multiply and mutate to become more virulent and our immune mechanism is depleted. We'd see plagues of typhoid, polio, dysentery . . . Things we've cured. They'd all come back. There would have to be large stockpiles of heroin and morphine to inject into the dying people. You can let your imagination wander a little bit and envision, generations later, the earth inhabited by bands of roving humanoids, unrecognizable as human beings. It will be the end of civilization—all the architecture, music, literature, art—and possibly, every organism on earth. There's real doubt whether any life would ultimately survive.

Q: In the fall of 1979 you visited the Soviet Union and met with a number of scientists, doctors, government officials, and everyday Russian citizens. What are their feelings about nuclear war?

A: Uniformly, every person we spoke to is very much against the arms race. They desperately wanted a freeze on the deployment of strategic nuclear weapons, desperately wanted SALT II ratified. They didn't want America to deploy the Cruise and Pershing missiles in Europe and they don't want China armed by America. They're frightened about nuclear war. They lost 20 million people in World War II and are very sensitive about war.

Q: After you returned from Russia you made some personal and professional decisions in response to the escalating arms race. What have you decided?

A: I'm giving up much of my medical work. I was about to start doing some interesting research in cystic fibrosis. Now I've decided not to do it. The decision really tore me apart, because I love what I'm doing. But I go to work and I just can't feel there's any point when there's a danger that every organism on earth will be destroyed in a couple of years.

Q: How do you keep from getting depressed when you face the realities of the nuclear nightmare so often?

A: Well, sometimes I do get depressed. When I was writing the chapter on nuclear weapons in my book *Nuclear Madness,* I became extremely depressed. I lived it and dreamt it, night after night. I saw bombs dropping out of planes; saw what the world would be like if there was a nuclear war and somehow my children and I survived. It was too terrible. But most of the time I practice what Robert Jay Lifton calls psychic numbing. He's the psychiatrist who worked with the survivors of Hiroshima and Nagasaki. Most of the time I don't think about it. I pretend that life will go on. I sew for the kids. I make cakes and look after the family. That's where my joy comes from—the family, the earth, other people. Life's a fantastic, precious thing. I don't think about it ending except when I write or talk about it.

Q: When you spoke of your personal nuclear nightmare, it made me think of Hiroshima. You were in Japan last year. What was that like for you?

A: I went to Hiroshima on the anniversary of the dropping of the bomb. The bomb was dropped at 8:15 in the morning on a hot, muggy summer day. We were in the Peace Park at exactly 8:15 when they released thousands of doves into the air. I was profoundly sad but at the same time I felt an intense anger. I thought of all the people who are still dying now from what they called A Bomb disease, but was in fact, cancer. The cancer incidence is still rising—35 years later. These bombs just don't kill people suddenly. They go on forever killing people. But we've learned nothing from that! In fact, I think we're hooked on nuclear weapons like a drug. We're paying for it with our taxes. Reverend William Sloane Coffin, who was one of the three clergy who visited the American hostages in Iran, and a member of the delegation that visited the Soviet Union, says it's like we're all sipping from the Pentagon Kool-Aid vat.

Q: Your working so hard on behalf of the planet and its peoples indicates a tremendous respect for the earth. Where does it come from?

A: When I studied medicine and I learned how the cells work, how the human body works—and how beautifully coordinated the whole thing is, it gave me a great reverence for life. When I had my own babies it was the most fantastically creative thing I ever did, giving birth. The babies cried and my breasts prickled with milk. The connection was even stronger. All women feel this potential creativity, I think, even if they've never given birth to a baby.

Q: So many people draw inspiration from your work to help them with their own efforts. What advice can you offer them to stay positive?

A: Well, I think in the face of catastrophe to do nothing and be passive is very depressing because you feel so powerless. But if you *try* and do something, it's the most exciting action you can take. If I'm feeling I'm having an effect and other people are starting to be mobilized, there's a *tremendous* reward. So I say to myself, "Even if the bombs go off, at least I'll be able to say I tried." For me, it's a religious commitment to continue evolution, to continue God's creation. We are the curators of life on earth. But with the press of a button, we can wipe it out.

"Waking America Up to the Nuclear Nightmare" is reprinted with permission of the author and *New Roots* Magazine, Box 548, Greenfield, Ma. 01302.

THE ARMS RACE OR THE HUMAN RACE

In pounds per person, the world has more explosive power than food. Since World War II, $4 trillion has been spent on the world arms race. While the nations of the world, led by the United States and the Soviet Union, spend over $500 billion a year (over $1 million a minute) on military programs, one billion people live on an average yearly income below $500. There are at least

660 million people in developing countries who cannot afford the basic necessities of life and thus live in subhuman poverty. Between 450 million and 750 million people in the developing countries of the world, more than the combined populations of the U.S. and the USSR, are seriously malnourished. In many affluent countries, an average of 10 percent of the population lives in abject poverty.

The massive expenditures on the arms race continue to increase daily while members of the human race suffer and die. Following are some concrete examples of how human needs could be met if the will and money spent on weapons were devoted to the interests of life.

—Malnutrition is the biggest single contributor to mortality in poorer countries. Children are the major victims. To eliminate hunger, both direct action and long-term development programs are needed. Two percent of the world's production of cereals would provide 500 additional calories a day to the seriously undernourished of the world.

Direct food aid for the hungry . . . $5 billion.

—An estimated two billion people in the world, most of them in developing nations, do not have access to a dependable, sanitary supply of water. Contaminated water is responsible for four out of five infectious diseases. Diarrheal diseases are the most common cause of death in young children.

Safe water for all within the decade . . . $4 billion.

—Half of the Third World population is without a minimum level of education. Primary education increases productivity, aids modernization and, from the national point of view, yields a higher return than any other form of investment. Additional school facilities are essential to increase enrollment.

Primary schools and teacher training . . . $5.5 billion.

—Malaria, which had dropped sharply after WHO launched a global campaign against it two decades ago, has again reached epidemic proportions. In Africa alone it is killing one million children a year. An effective program requires the draining of swamps, pesticides, antimalarial drugs, and a new vaccine.

Global program to wipe out malaria . . . $2 billion.

—Throughout the world there is a shortage of trained medical personnel in rural and poor areas. A growing number of elderly persons are dependent on neighborhood health care. Primary health care systems, using small health facilities and medical auxiliaries, can ensure better health protection and preventive medicine in both affluent and poor countries.

Primary health care facilities and personnel . . . $1.5 billion.

—In the developing world, 15 million children die in a single year, many killed by diseases such as diphtheria, tetanus, measles, poliomyelitis, that have been virtually eliminated in developed countries through immunization programs.

Vaccine protection for all children . . . $500 million.

—Only a small fraction of abundant reserves of hydroelectric power in developing nations is now being utilized. Fuel wood is consumed at a rate which threatens a wood famine in the foreseeable future. Reforestation, bioconversion, small dams, low-cost solar devices could reduce dependence on oil, and help to meet growing energy needs.

Development of renewable energy resources . . . $3 billion.

—There are 50 million new entrants in the labor force each year. Lack of training in basic and technical skills blocks job opportunities for many young people, increases unemployment, slows national economic growth.

Training programs for young people . . . $4 billion.

© World Military and Social Expenditures, 1979.

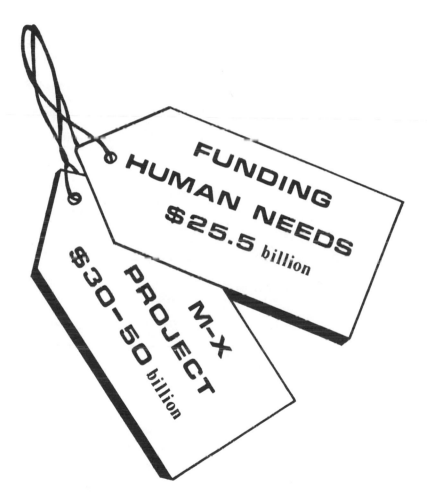

DO YOU KNOW WHAT YOUR TAX DOLLAR BUYS?

Much of your tax dollar gets to pay for wars—past, present, and future. In fact, the U.S. has spent $1.8 trillion on the military since the end of World War II.

The Carter Administration has requested $696 billion in federal funds for fiscal 1981. Of this amount:

Military: 47%: Some *32% of the budget* is earmarked for current military expenditures and 15% for the cost of past wars. Of the costs of past wars, 5% is for veterans benefits, and 10% for interest on the national debt, two-thirds of which can be conservatively estimated as war-incurred.

This military percentage of the federal funds budget does not include the following items, portions of which could arguably be viewed as military related: NASA, Coast Guard, naval petroleum reserves, part of school assistance to federally impacted areas, the Commerce Department subsidy to ships for the National Defense Fleet, and others.

Human Resources (education, manpower, social services, health, income security): 29%.

Physical Resources (agriculture, community, and regional development, natural resources, commerce, transportation, environment, energy): 11%.

All other (international affairs, justice, space, general government, revenue-sharing, and one-fourth of the interest on the national debt): 13%.

(Source: SANE; figures compiled by the Women's International League for Peace and Freedom [WILPF] Legislative Office.)

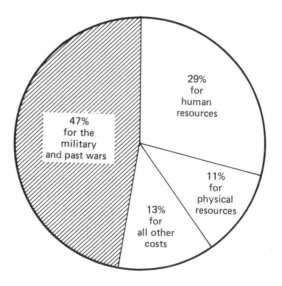

CONVERTING FROM MILITARY TO PEACE PRODUCTION

Direct and Indirect Jobs Generated by One Billion Dollars in Final Demand in Various Economic Sectors.

Economic Sector	*Average Number of Jobs per Billion Dollars of Demand*
Military: includes aircraft, electronics, ordinance, missiles, petroleum products, shipbuilding and repairs.	76,000 jobs
Machinery: includes farm, metal-working and general industrial machinery.	86,000 jobs
Transportation: includes railroad, local, and intercity transit and transportation equipment.	92,000 jobs
Construction: includes housing rehabilitation, new residential housing, public utilities, and general maintenance and repair work.	100,000 jobs
Personal Consumption: resulting from a $1 billion tax cut, includes retail and wholesale trade, food products, motor vehicles, clothing, petroleum products, communications and personal service sectors.	112,000 jobs
Health: includes services, hospitals, and instruments.	139,000 jobs
Education: includes educational services.	187,000 jobs

Source: U.S. Bureau of Labor Statistics, as cited in "Priorities," June 1976.

"Refusal to undertake this conversion [of military-related industries to peace-oriented industries] is completely incompatible with the spirit of humanity and still more with the spirit of Christianity" because "it is unthinkable that no other work can be found for hundreds of thousands of workers than the production of instruments of death."

(From Pope Paul VI, speech to the Diplomatic Corps, February 10, 1972.)

APPENDIX 5

Responding as Church to the Nuclear Arms Race

Taking Action for Peace · 100

Letter from Father Thomas Merton to James Forest · 101

Groups Working for Disarmament and Social Justice · 103

Resources · 108

TAKING ACTION FOR PEACE

Acting as faith communities in response to the moral and spiritual problems of our day is what being church is all about. These personal, intentional Christian communities constitute the vibrant and hopeful church of our day, a phenomenon often unseen by those who view church merely as institution. The responsibility of our faith belongs to such communities as these, as it once did to the community of twelve around Jesus: to live and proclaim the gospel.

As church in a nuclear society, our communities bear the particular responsibility to challenge and reverse the nuclear arms race and the values that support it in the name of the gospel. Such an undertaking may cause us to wonder if we are still only twelve in number. The task is extraordinarily immense. However, it is the faith aspect of our communities that enables us to let God measure the worth of our action rather than to measure it ourselves. Prayer is the ultimate expression of this faith; it keeps us both hopeful and modest. Action based in open prayer and a common faith offers a greater promise and endurance than normal expectation would allow. This dynamic relation of prayer and action is integral to the response that true discipleship demands of us.

A large part of our peace ministry as church consists in educating and raising consciousness about the nuclear arms race. The conflict of Kingdom and worldly values in our culture is immediately evident in the way in which the question of nuclear weapons is generally considered in government and in the mass media. The human life issue, it seems, is almost always lost in the debate about international and domestic economic and political matters. These matters are not unimportant, but the question of the values of human life is absolutely primary for the Christian disciple. Our efforts at educating ourselves and others should reflect this priority of values. Prayerful reflection on what we have heard or said, and have learned, is vital—it is easy to be overwhelmed by the sheer volume of data available on the subject of nuclear weapons.

The small, simple and obvious means of educating are the ones we recommend. Education on such a personal basis often implies a level of commitment and sometimes risk which tends by itself to be persuasive. Examples of educational efforts include: encouraging and developing prayer and study groups that focus on the nuclear arms race problem; gathering friends and neighbors in your home for discussion or viewing a film; distributing literature at churches, schools, and work sites; writing letters to members of Congress as well as to editors of the local secular and religious press; encouraging local clergy to acquaint their congregations with particular church statements against the nuclear arms race; relating to other individuals and communities in the region similarly engaged in peace and social justice work, perhaps through a network of churches.

Undertaking research on local war industry contracts helps to illustrate the extent to which the nuclear arms race concretely affects our own cities and towns as well as the jobs they offer. A good source of data for such a project is the National Action/Research on the Military-Industrial Complex

100

68,029

(NARMIC), which can provide a list of annual military contract awards for each county in the United States. Also available is a list of contracts awarded to individual companies.

Social action for justice and peace is a constitutive element of the gospel mandate. The link between the concerns of justice and peace are found in the economic basis of war itself as well as in the effects of war in our society and in the world—namely, poverty. The nuclear arms race has produced enormous poverty both morally and materially in society. As followers of Jesus who identify with the poor and the oppressed, we are obliged to deal with the poverty around us: to serve its victims, to work toward the elimination of its causes, and in some ways to make it our own.

Addressing the problems of human need locally by responding to them in personal service constitutes an important witness against the nuclear arms race. Such action not only serves its indirect victims but also exposes in human terms the priority given to war-making systems rather than to life-supporting systems in our culture. Providing emergency housing, working in a soup kitchen or halfway house, or other forms of voluntary service are examples of this type of action. Another example would be for a faith community or congregation to house and financially support a worker who has left war-related employment for reasons of conscience.

Coupled with these healing forms of action is the radical witness of nonviolent protest and resistance. This type of action follows in the tradition of Jesus' cleansing of the temple. Examples would include: helping to develop a disarmament and peace conversion campaign organized around a local nuclear weapons research or production plant; organizing public liturgies, vigils for peace, or demonstrations at local Congressional offices or at a nuclear weapons plant; engaging in nonviolent civil disobedience at such locations; resisting the payment of the portion of one's federal taxes used to finance the military budget; and leaving a military research or production job for reasons of faith and conscience.

There are many, many more ideas for church action for peace. The national and local groups listed in this Appendix and the educational resources recommended in the next one may be helpful in providing you with more information and ideas. We would not, of course, presume to offer an exhaustive list of possible suggestions for action; our modest hope here is to help stimulate discussion and planning for action in your own faith community. An openness to the working of the Spirit will inform your action choices as well as the actions themselves. Developing a peace ministry is a fragile and vulnerable struggle; yet out of this struggle and Cross experience emerges new life and hope.

LETTER FROM FATHER THOMAS MERTON
TO JAMES FOREST

Do not depend on the hope of results. When you are doing the sort of work you have taken on, essentially an apostolic work, you may have to face the fact that your work will be apparently worthless and even achieve no result at all, if not perhaps results opposite to what you expect. As you get used to this idea, you start more and more to concentrate not on the results but on the value, the rightness, the truth of the work itself. And there too a great deal has to be gone through, as gradually you struggle less and less for an idea and more and more for specific people. The range tends to narrow down, but it gets much more real. In the end, it is the reality of personal relationships that saves everything.

You are fed up with words, and I don't blame you. I am nauseated by them sometimes. I am also, to tell the truth, nauseated by ideals and with causes. This sounds like heresy, but I think you will understand what I mean. It is so easy to get engrossed with ideas and slogans and myths that in the end one is left holding the bag, empty, with no trace of meaning left in it. And then the temptation is to yell louder than ever in order to make the meaning be there again by magic. Going through this kind of reaction helps you to guard against this. Your system is complaining of too much verbalizing, and it is right.

. . . the big results are not in your hands or mine, but they suddenly happen, and we can share in them; but there is no point in building our lives on this personal satisfaction which may be denied us and which after all is not that important.

The next step in the process is for you to see that your own thinking about what you are doing is crucially important. You are probably striving to build yourself an identity in your work, out of your work and your witness. You are using it, so to speak, to protect yourself against nothingness, annihilation. That is not the right use of your work. All the good that you will do will come not from you but from the fact that you have allowed yourself, in the obedience of faith, to be used by God's love. Think of this more and gradually you will be free from the need to prove yourself, and you can be more open to the power that will work through you without your knowing it.

The great thing after all is to live, not to pour out your life in the service of a myth: and we turn the best things into myths. If you can get free from the domination of causes and just serve Christ's truth, you will be able to do more and will be less crushed by the inevitable disappointments. Because I see nothing whatever in sight but much disappointment, frustration, and confusion . . .

The real hope, then, is not in something we think we can do, but in God who is making something good out of it in some way we cannot see. If we can do His will, we will be helping in this process. But we will not necessarily know all about it beforehand . . .

Enough of this . . . it is at least a gesture . . . I will keep you in my prayers.

All the best in Christ,
Tom

Thomas Merton, who died in 1968, was a Trappist monk, priest, spiritual writer and a prophetic voice for peace, disarmament, and social justice. James

Forest, a former editor of *Catholic Worker*, is now the coordinator of the International Fellowship of Reconciliation, a worldwide ecumenical pacifist organization based in Holland. (Reprinted by permission of James Forest.)

GROUPS WORKING ON NATIONAL AND LOCAL LEVELS FOR DISARMAMENT AND SOCIAL JUSTICE

American Friends Service Committee (AFSC) 1501 Cherry St. Philadelphia, PA. 19102.

Works to build informed resistance to war and militarism and to advance nonviolent action for change. Publishes a wide variety of resources on peace and disarmament.

Catholic Worker 36 E. First St. New York, NY. 10012.

The oldest of the over fifty existing Catholic Worker communities in the U.S. that is committed to the "works of mercy and peace" from a gospel-pacifist perspective. Publishes a monthly newspaper.

Center on Law and Pacifism Box 1584 Colorado Springs, CO. 80901

Focuses on legal counseling for war tax resistance and provides information on conscientious objection in the nuclear age.

Center for Defense Information (CDI) 122 Maryland Ave., N.E. Washington, DC. 20002.

CDI conducts extensive research and public education on U.S. military policies. Publishes monthly newsletter called "Defense Monitor."

Clergy and Laity Concerned (CALC) 198 Broadway New York, NY. 10038.

An interfaith organization dedicated to religious political action for justice and peace. Distributes a 24-page guide, "Worship and Action Resources for a Non-Nuclear Future," along with a wide range of other disarmament-justice resources.

Coalition For a New Foreign and Military Policy 120 Maryland Ave., N.E. Washington, DC. 20002.

A coalition of social action, religious, labor, and peace groups working for a peaceful, demilitarized U.S. foreign policy. Distributes a variety of disarmament resources.

Covenant Peace Community
66 Edgewood Ave.
New Haven, CT. 06511

A gospel-based community in Connecticut working for nuclear disarmament and social justice. Affiliated with the Atlantic Life Community.

Fellowship of Reconciliation
Box 271
Nyack, NY. 10960.

A pacifist group working for disarmament and social change. Has many local and denominational fellowships. Publishes *Fellowship,* a monthly magazine.

Global Education Associates
552 Park Ave.
East Orange, N.J. 07117

An interfaith educational organization working nationally and internationally for world justice. Publishes a variety of curriculum resources for schools and study groups on justice and peace issues.

Great Lakes Life Community
Contact: Day House
2640 Trumbull
Detroit, MI. 48216.

A community of groups and individuals in the Michigan area who are committed to nonviolent resistance to the Trident program and all forms of militarism.

Ground Zero: Center for Nonviolent Action
Rt. 5, Box 5423
Poulsbo, WA. 98370.

Organizing base for the nonviolent campaign to halt construction of the Trident submarine base which is being built in the Puget Sound area of Bangor, Washington.

Institute for Defense and Disarmament Studies (IDDS)
251 Harvard St.
Brookline, MA. 02146.

A research and public education center studying the nature and purposes of military forces. Publishes the *American Peace Directory* which includes 2,000 national and local peace groups.

Institute for Policy Studies (IPS)
901 Q St. N.W.
Washington, DC. 20009.

A research and public education organization concerned with international issues including disarmament. Publishes books and other materials on disarmament.

Institute for World Order
777 United Nations Plaza
New York, NY. 10017.

Produces written and audiovisual resources on the arms race.

International Fellowship of
Reconciliation (IFOR)
Hof van Sonoy 15-17
1811 D, Alkmaar
The Netherlands.

A transnational religious community
of different faiths committed to
nonviolence as a principle of life for
a world community of peace and
liberation. Has affiliates in 30
countries and publishes a monthly
magazine, with a strong focus on
human rights and disarmament,
called *IFOR Report.*

Jonah House
1933 Park Ave.
Baltimore, MD. 21217.

A gospel-based community
committed to nonviolent resistance
against the nuclear arms race.
Contact for the Atlantic Life
Community, which is a network of
East Coast resistance communities
involved in nonviolent campaigns at
the Pentagon, White House, and
nuclear weapons facilities. Publishes
a regular newsletter called "Year
One."

Mobilization For Survival (MFS)
3601 Locust Walk
Philadelphia, PA. 19104.

A coalition of groups which
emphasizes grass-roots organization
and action toward reversing the arms
race and halting nuclear power
plants. The Religious Task Force of
the MFS is actively involved in
organizing in the religious
community around the same goals. It
is a clearinghouse for an array of
antinuclear resources including an
audiovisual guide.

National Action/Research on the
Military-Industrial Complex
(NARMIC)
1501 Cherry St.
Philadelphia, PA. 19102.

A project of AFSC, provides
educational resources on U.S.
foreign policy and local military
contracting including "Arming for
the 80's," a series of military-
industrial maps and "How to
Research Your Local War
Industry."

National Citizens' Hearings
for Radiation Victims
317 Pennsylvania Ave., S.E.
Washington, DC., 20003.

An organization that focuses on
radiation hazards related to the
nuclear industry. Offers slide shows
and other resources on radiation.

National Inter-religious Service Board for Conscientious Objectors (NISBCO)
550 Washington Building
15th and New York Ave., N.W.
Washington, DC. 20005.

A coalition of religious groups who oppose all forms of registration, the draft, or compulsory national service. Provides resources on countering military recruiting and on draft counseling, including a booklet on Religious Statements on Conscientious Objection.

Pacific Life Community
631 Kiely Boulevard
Santa Clara, CA. 95051.

A network of West Coast resistance communities involved in a nonviolent campaign to stop the Trident program. PLC is helping to build a transnational community of nonviolent resistance against nuclear weapons with the peoples of the Pacific. Ground Zero is another contact for this group. Publishes a regular newsletter.

Pax Christi
3000 North Mango Ave.
Chicago, IL. 60634.

A national Catholic pacifist organization involved in acting for and educating about peacemaking and nuclear disarmament. Distributes Catholic-oriented resources on peace and disarmament.

Physicians for Social Responsibility (PSR)
Box 295
Cambridge, MA. 02236.

A group of health and medical professionals who provide information about the health hazards of nuclear weaponry and nuclear power.

Riverside Church Program
490 Riverside Drive
New York, NY. 10027.

Provides speakers and resources for local disarmament education, particularly for the religious community. Published book, *Peace In Search of Makers*. Distributes a religious slide show on disarmament and publishes a regular newsletter.

Rocky Flats/Nuclear Weapons Facilities Project
FOR/AFSC
1428 Lafayette St.
Denver, CO. 80218.

Information on projects around the country, especially Rocky Flats Nuclear Facility, that organize action to convert local nuclear weapons facilities to socially useful production. Distributes an Organizing Packet.

SANE
514 C St., N.E.
Washington, DC. 20002.

Mobilizes grass-roots initiatives for peace and disarmament, with emphasis on planned economic conversion. Publishes "The Conversion Planner." Also distributes a newsletter and other resources.

Stockholm International Peace
Research Institute (SIPRI)
Sveavugen 166, S-113 46
Stockholm, Sweden.

An independent institute for research into problems of peace and conflict and disarmament. For a list of SIPRI publications write: MIT Press, 28 Carleton St., Cambridge, MA. 02142.

Sojourners
1309 L St., N.W.
Washington, DC. 20005.

A Christian Evangelical community working for church renewal, social justice, and nuclear disarmament. Publishes a monthly magazine. Contact Peace Ministries for religious-oriented disarmament resources, including a new book on the nuclear arms race and the religious community.

U.S. Catholic Conference
Office of International Justice and
Peace
1312 Massachusetts Ave., N.W.
Washington, DC. 20005.

Addresses the issues of the arms race within the context of church teachings. Distributes materials on this subject.

War Resisters League (WRL)
339 Lafayette St.
New York, NY. 10012.

A national pacifist group that opposes armaments, conscription, and war; it relates the problem of war to economic and social justice. Publishes "WRL News" bimonthly and *WIN* magazine.

Women's International League
for Peace and Freedom (WILPF)
1213 Race St.
Philadelphia, PA. 19107.

An international organization which emphasizes nonviolent solutions to domestic and international problems. Works actively on disarmament issues. Publishes "Peace and Freedom Newsletters" and other resources.

Women Strike for Peace (WSP)
145 South 13 St.
Philadelphia, PA. 19107.

A group of women dedicated to achieving international disarmament under effective controls. They work to ban nuclear testing and to end the arms race. Publishes newsletters, leaflets, and action alerts.

World Peacemakers
2852 Ontario Road, N.W.
Washington, DC. 20009.

A religious-political oriented group working for World Peace. Publishes "World Peace" papers and a "Handbook for World Peacemaker Groups."

RESOURCES

Books on Reversing the Arms Race, Nonviolence, and Christian Pacifism

Aldridge, Robert J. *The Counterforce Syndrome: A Guide to U.S. Nuclear Weapons and Strategic Doctrine* (Washington, D.C.: Transnational Institute, 1978).

Bainton, Ronald H. *Christian Attitudes Towards War and Peace* (Nashville: Abingdon Press, 1960).

Barnet, Richard. *Roots of War* (Baltimore: Penguin Books, 1971).

——— *The Giants: Russia and America* (New York: Simon & Schuster, 1977).

Berrigan, Daniel. *Uncommon Prayer* (New York: Seabury Press, 1978).

Berrigan, Philip. *Of Beasts and Other Beastly Images: Essays Under the Bomb* (Portland, Ore.: Sunburst Press, 1978).

Boston Study Group. *The Price of Defense* (New York: Times Books, 1979).

Caldicott, Helen. *Nuclear Madness: What You Can Do* (Brookline, Mass.: Autumn Press, 1978).

Cooney, Robert and Michalowski, Helen (Eds.). *The Power of the People: Active Nonviolence in the U.S.* (Culver City, Calif.: Peace Press, 1977).

Del Vasto, Lanza. *Warriors of Peace* (New York: Alfred A. Knopf, 1974).

Donaghy, John and Osterle, William H. *Peace Theology and the Arms Race: Readings in Arms and Disarmament* (Philadelphia: College Theology Society Publications, 1980).

Douglass, James W. *The Non-Violent Cross: A Theology of Revolution & Peace* (New York: Macmillan, 1969).

——— *Resistance and Contemplation: The Way of Liberation* (New York: Dell Publishing, 1972).

Ferguson, John. *The Politics of Love—The New Testament and Non-Violent Revolution* (Greenwood, S.C.: The Attic Press, 1976).

Gandhi, M. K. *Non-Violent Resistance* (New York: Schocken Books, 1967).

Guinan, Edward. *Peace and Nonviolence* (New York: Paulist Press, 1973).

Lens, Sidney. *The Day Before Doomsday: An Anatomy of the Nuclear Arms Race* (Boston: Beacon Press, 1977).

Lifton, Robert J. *Death in Life—Survivors of Hiroshima* (New York: Simon & Schuster, 1967).

McSorley, Richard. *Kill? For Peace?* (Washington, D.C.: Center for Peace Studies, Georgetown University, 1978)

——— *New Testament Basis of Peacemaking* (Washington, D.C.: Center for Peace Studies, Georgetown University, 1979).

Melman, Seymour. *The Permanent War Economy* (New York: Simon & Schuster, 1974).

Merton, Thomas. *Faith and Violence* (Notre Dame, Ind.: University of Notre Dame Press, 1968).

Rockman, Jane (Ed.). *Peace in Search of Makers: Riverside Church Reverse the Arms Race Convocation* (Valley Forge, Pa.: Judson Press, 1979).

Sampson, Anthony. *The Arms Bazaar: From Lebanon to Lockheed* (New York: Bantam Books, 1973).

Sharp, Gene. *The Politics of Nonviolent Action* (Boston: Porter Sargent Publisher, 1973).

Shelly, Maynard. *New Call for Peacemakers: A New Call to Peacemaking Study Guide* (Newton, Kan.: Faith and Life Press, 1979).

Stringfellow, William. *An Ethic for Christians and Other Aliens in a Strange Land* (Waco, Tex.: World Books Publisher, 1973).

——— *Conscience and Obedience* (Waco, Tex.: World Books Publisher, 1977).

Yoder, John H. *The Politics of Jesus* (Grand Rapids, Mich.: Eerdmans, 1972).

Zahn, Gordon. *In Solitary Witness* (Boston: Beacon Press, 1964).

Periodicals

Articles on the arms race can be found in many periodicals including *America, Bulletin of the Atomic Scientists, Christian Century, Christianity in Crisis, Commonweal, The Nation, National Catholic Reporter, Mother Jones, New Age, New Roots, The Progressive,* and *Scientific American.*

Audiovisual Resources

The slide shows and films listed below are excellent educational tools on various aspects of the nuclear arms race. For a complete listing of other available audiovisual aids on the nuclear arms race contact the Mobilization for Survival for their antinuclear audiovisual guide. (See Groups Listing)

"Atomic Age: A Trail of Victims"—A 20-minute slide presentation on the plight of people who have been exposed to radiation from nuclear technology. Fellowship of Reconciliation, Box 271, Nyack, N.Y. 10960.

"Conscience and War Taxes"—A 20-minute slide show on the conscientious opposition to taxes used for war and military purposes. National Council for a World Peace Tax Fund, 2111 Florida Ave. N.W., Washington, D.C. 20008.

"Hiroshima/Nagasaki"—Films depicting the 1945 atomic destruction of these two Japanese cities. Wilmington College, Wilmington, Ohio 45177.

"Last Slide Show"—Traces military history to the present nuclear threat and promotes the goals of the Mobilization for Survival. (See Groups Listing)

"Mr. Nixon's Secret Legacy"—A 30-minute film produced by the BBC in 1974 on U.S. "counterforce" capability as well as a series of interviews with people who are prepared to comply with orders to unleash nuclear weapons. Mennonite Central Committee, 21 S. 12 St., Akron, Pa. 17501.

"Paul Jacobs and the Nuclear Gang"—A film about how civilians and soldiers were exposed to the atomic tests of the 1950s with a particular focus on Paul Jacobs, a journalist, who after a long illness of leukemia, died in 1978. Film Donnelly/Colt, Box 271, New Vernon, N.J. 07976.

"War Without Winners"—A-30 minute film on the need to reverse the arms race from an American and a Soviet perspective. Produced by the Center for Defense Information. Available from the CDI or Films, Inc. 733 Green Bay Road, Wilmette, Ill. 60091. (See Groups Listing)